Women and Political Issues

(An International Perspective)

Women and Political Issues

(An International Perspective)

Vaikunth Mehta

ABD PUBLISHERS

Jaipur ■ New Delhi

ABD PUBLISHERS

Regd. Off. "Bony Residency", Gate No. 2
Opp. Tilak Public School, Vishweswariya Nagar,
Gopalpura Road, Jaipur - 302018, India
Ph: 0141 - 2761280, Telefax: 2761381
Email: abdpublishersjpr@gmail.com

Delhi Office: 102, 1st Floor, Satyam House,
4327/3, Ansari Road, Darya Ganj,
New Delhi - 110002, India
Ph: 011-45652440

visit us: www.oxfordbookcompany.com

Published in India, 2024

ISBN : 9788183760465

Price : ₹ 1575/-

Typeset by Shivangi Computer, Jaipur

Printed and bound in India by Thomson Press Ltd.,
New Delhi

Preface

Though born equal, women all over the world were subjected to social, political, economic, cultural and opportunity discriminations. The condition of women in developing countries was more pathetic as they were even subjected to brutalism and barbarism. Though they worked harder than their male counterparts, yet they were not given economic freedom. In social and cultural fields, women were discriminated and were not allowed to participate in certain activities. Women in both developed and developing countries were not provided equal opportunities for employment and even if they happened to get employment they were discriminated in wages and given less emoluments than men for same work. Being illiterate, most of them were denied political rights such as right to vote. Thus, discrimination and inequality became their lot.

American women started protesting against such male attitude since the beginning of 20th century and succeeded in getting right of suffrage which enabled the them to participate in the political decisions of the nation. After World War II, the political objective of equal treatment seemed more within reach much due to liberalism of Kennedy Administration and ultimately Equal Rights Amendment and President's Commission on Status of Women became centrepiece for achievement of equal rights for women. These along with other legislations were the government action that ultimately resulted in providing equal status to women.

The present empowered status of women in human society is the result of a long fight undertook by many women activists. The book makes elaborate discussion on who these women were, what they wanted to achieve, what was their agenda for equal rights, how they fought for their rights and what rights they achieved. The book makes presentment of their political strategies and outcomes.

Vaikunth Mehta

Contents

1

Equal Pay Legislation

The cardinal premise of the Women's Bureau coalition held that the Equal Rights Amendment would do little to help women; discrimination could be eliminated only by the prudent enactment of "specific bills for specific ills." The "specific bill" offered by ERA opponents in 1945 sought to protect equal pay for equal work for women in private employment. Such a strategy possessed several advantages: it gave opponents of the ERA a positive goal rather than a negative one; it took advantage of the wartime impulse to recognise the contribution of women in jobs traditionally done by men; it allowed a focus on unfair practices that genuinely harmed women and their families, sidelining discussion about whether "theoretical" statements of equality were of value; it proposed a change in the law that was less unsettling than the ERA because it was so much narrower; and it placed ERA adversaries squarely in favour of eliminating discrimination.

But this bill faced a major problem in the postwar world. Higher wage rates would draw more women into the workforce, not encourage them to stay home. Thus the impulse to reward women for their wartime efforts ran counter to another current:

the fear that returning soldiers would face job shortages. Making it more lucrative for women to stay in the workforce would hinder men's efforts to find jobs. Moreover, federal support, in the form of legislation guaranteeing equal opportunity in the workplace would appear to confirm the social shifts the war had produced. The war had made working women visible—and that visibility made people nervous. The fight for equal pay once again played out the tension between institutionalising the wartime gains of women in the public arena and reinstalling them as keepers of the hearth.

In addition, the quest for equal pay legislation was hampered by the ERA struggle. Because it had been proposed by ERA opponents, some advocates of the amendment viewed the legislation with suspicion. The ERA continued to be the chief legislative goal of the groups that favoured it, and the primary supporters of equal pay never devoted equivalent resources to getting their bill through. The split between the pro- and anti-ERA forces made it more difficult for women to overcome both the "back to the home" sentiment and the conservative animus against business regulation in general.

By the end of the following decade, however, both the economic and the social context had changed. Women had clearly become a permanent part of the labour force—bound securely to women's jobs. The expanding peacetime economy, in fact, had created more service and clerical jobs than ever before, so employers welcomed—indeed, sought—women workers. In assuming these jobs, women continued to bear the major responsibility for their families' welfare, so the burden on husbands of working wives was small. With the newly generated need for women workers, the sentiment in favour of equal pay legislation began to grow, and it soon stood a real chance of passage. But social and economic supports were necessary, not sufficient, conditions. Real success required a more favourable political situation.

In the postwar period, President Truman gave the reformers seeking an equal pay law reason to believe he would support such an effort. After assuming office on Franklin Roosevelt's death, he made clear gestures to identify himself with his predecessor's liberal programme, designed to encourage growth and progress in the postwar period. He promoted national health insurance and aid to education and, in particular, took a stand against discrimination by issuing executive orders banning prejudicial actions against black Americans in the civil service and in the military. Such efforts made it plain that discrimination against any group in the United States—even women—could be combated through federal measures.

At the same time, though, the government had focused its sights on trying to cap the skyrocketing inflation rate and maximising the employment of former GIs. Yet President Truman seemed unable to craft an effective programme to meet these needs, or to deal with labour unrest that led to strikes in the steel, automobile, electric, coal, maritime, and railroad industries. In the 1946 elections Republicans took control of both houses of Congress for the first time in fourteen years. The Taft-Hartley Act, passed over the president's veto in June 1947, circumscribed the right of unions to control hiring. Policy goals sought to keep wage rates down and the employment of males up. Nevertheless, women activists in Washington, interested in advancing women's status even while maintaining "reasonable distinctions" between the sexes, worked to raise women's wages and assert their right to jobs.

The quest began in February 1945 when the National Committee to Defeat the Unequal Rights Amendment drafted a bill to be introduced by Senators Wayne Morse (R-Oreg.) and Claude Pepper (D-Fla.). NCDURA's desire to eliminate a prevalent and serious problem for women workers was genuine, and it solicited the backing of all women's organisations, both favourable to and hostile toward the ERA. In order to separate equal pay from its opposition to the ERA, NCDURA established an independent national equal pay committee, which the pro-ERA BPW quickly agreed to join.

But however sincere the motives of supporters of equal pay,

the impetus for the measure was the desire to divert attention from the ERA. NCDURA counselled its members to urge legislators to vote both in favour of the equal pay bill and against the ERA, and Mary Anderson, the ERA's archfoe (who had resigned the year before, at age seventy-two, as director of the Women's Bureau) herself chaired the new equal pay committee and drew up the bill. The bill thus got hit from two sides—by those who favoured the ERA and did not want what they saw as a more important effort vitiated by a narrower one, and by those who opposed any interference in the workplace and wanted no law at all.

Often both these opponents were conservatives, either Republicans or conservative Democrats. Although the liberal-conservative split was muddled in the Era battle, on the question of equal pay it stood out clearly. Equal pay legislation came out of the protective labour law tradition, and the original version of the bill protected only women's wage rates. Liberal organisations lined up behind the bill, but conservatives who supported independent free enterprise opposed an equal pay law. Those conservatives who also supported the ERA thus had two "good" reasons to fight equal pay legislation.

In proposing to protect women's wage rates, the liberals were arguing not in favour of new roles for women but for recognising the reality, however undesirable it might be, of women in the workforce. Working women had taken jobs because they needed the money. Equity and decency demanded that employers pay them a fair wage—that is, the rate a man earned for the same job.

The argument might have carried the day, but in drafting the bill, Anderson, never politically astute, ignored important political considerations and made several inflammatory moves. She modelled the bill after the sweeping coverage of the National Labour Relations Act, which applied to employers engaged in businesses "affecting" commerce, rather than following the narrower coverage of the Fair Labour Standards Act, which applied only to those actually participating in interstate commerce. The bill protected the pay only of women; a man earning less than a woman at a particular job (assuming such a person existed) had no recourse. Although not important from a practical point of view, the exclusion of men from the law's protection gave the bill's opponents a powerful "equal treatment" argument to use against it. The bill also forbade employers to discharge women without cause, a provision intended to help women keep wartime employment (a goal few endorsed in 1945). Anderson went so far as to vest enforcement power in the director of the Women's Bureau. A fact-finding agency, the bureau had never had this kind of enforcement authority and had no machinery to perform it. The provision of the bill that sparked the most opposition provided for an "advisory committee" that would establish wage differentials among different types of work. Opponents could thus contend that the bureau had aims completely apart from the mere protection of women's wage rates. Finally, the bill permitted the blacklisting of employers found guilty of wage discrimination, a red flag to business interests whose cooperation the bill's supporters needed. Said one partisan, in something of an understatement: "With the enactment of this law, we will be entering[an] . . . unchartered [*sic*] field."

The chances for some kind of equal pay legislation looked promising because of patriotic sentiment in its favour and because studies done during World War II had documented an authentic problem of widespread wage discrimination. "Women in producing the weapons of war have, in many industries and occupations, demonstrated their ability to turn out the same day's work as do men", Senators Pepper and Morse asserted when they introduced Anderson's bill; employers should not treat them like "second class workmen". The Women's Bureau representatives had indeed discovered a large war plant where women instructors got sixty cents an hour, whereas the men they were teaching received seventy cents. In the small arms and artillery ammunition plants the bureau representatives visited, entering wage rates were found to be at least ten cents an hour higher for men than for women; in gun manufacturing men began at sixteen cents an hour more. The *New York Herald Tribune* pointed to the war widows, now the sole support of their families, and urged no further delay of "so just a measure" as the equal pay bill.

Congress responded apathetically. Mary Norton (D-N.J.), chairman of the House Labour Committee, told Women's Bureau director Frieda Miller that no legislation would be enacted without an active campaign revealing "intense interest" on the part of women's organisations, labour unions, and the administration. In response, Mary Anderson expanded the equal pay committee she had formed, now called the National Committee on Equal Pay. Labour and women's organisations came on board, and the CIO replied: "[We] are anxious to work with you."

Not surprisingly, the National Woman's party hung back. Its response to a Supreme Court decision in 1936 on a wage and hour case had revealed its antipathy to labour legislation in general: now, although it declined to oppose this bill overtly, its members complained to congressional backers about several of the bill's features. They objected first to a special bill pertaining only to women rather than mandating equal pay for equal work regardless of sex. But even more, they rejected the bureau as the law's enforcement agent. As the chairman of the National Advisory Council of the NWP, Nora Stanton Barney, wrote to Senator Claude Pepper: "We do not want women to have any more legislation setting them apart from other workers, and sincerely wish the Women's Bureau did not exist. We certainly do not want it given any more power over the lives of women." The party feared that, at worst, Anderson's plan would work and Congress, instead of enacting the Equal Rights Amendment, would use equal pay legislation to mollify women.

Equal pay advocates took no pains to conceal this possibility; indeed, they regarded it as a selling point. Elizabeth Magee, general secretary of the National Consumers League, issued a press release observing that the equal pay bill "may lead to the shelving of the proposed Equal Rights Amendment," and Dorothy McAllister, the head of NCDURA, told her committee members that passage of the equal pay bill "would greatly weaken the interest some Senators have in the [Equal Rights] Amendment".

At the end of October 1945, the Senate Education and Labour Committee held hearings on the bill. Labour unions, including the AFL, offered support, as did the administration in the person of the secretary of labour. (The president said he endorsed the "principle" but no particular bill.) Speakers emphasised equity, the protection of wage rates for male workers, the needs of widows, and postwar purchasing power to sustain the economy. The BPW and the General Federation of Women's Clubs spoke in favour, also emphasising their support of the ERA, and the NWP kept mum. No one testified against the bill.

The committee took seven months to report the bill. It had eliminated the provision against firing women (even Frieda Miller had testified against this provision) and vested enforcement in the secretary of labour. Even so, labour subcommittee chairman James Tunnel (D-Del.) seemed only mildly interested in the bill, and committee members Robert Taft (R-Ohio) and Joseph Ball (R-Mich.), who had strong business constituents and conservative economic principles, opposed it. The measure did have a good friend on the House side however. Mary Norton saw to it that in July the House Labour Committee, which she chaired, reported a similar bill, without hearings to create delay.

The bill went no further. Because the Senate committee had taken so long, the bill reached the Senate floor near the close of the session. Robert Taft took to the floor against hasty consideration: "The bill involves a major interference with the freedom of American industry. Certainly it ought not to come up during the last days of the session." With the assistance of Joe Ball, who leapt to his defense against charges of indifference to women's rights, they scuttled the measure for 1946.

This first defeat undid the bill. The ERA had gone down

the previous July, so the chief impetus for the coalition backing equal pay legislation had withered. The wartime contributions of women were beginning to fade from memory, as was the desire to reward those efforts. Sympathetic Congress members continued to introduce the bill, but without an outside lobbying effort the cause was futile. In subsequent hearings industry lobbyists, emboldened no doubt by the earlier failure, argued that federal legislation was unnecessary and intrusive—a position supported, to the dismay of equal pay advocates, by the AFL. The labour federation had reversed its position in 1947, arguing that collective bargaining was a more effective tool for securing pay equity for women, a position it took despite the fact that many labour unions continued to include dual pay scales in their contracts.

With the Korean conflict some supporters became hopeful that Congress would use equal pay to encourage women to do war work. Mary Norton, now in the Department of Labour, asked Representative John F. Kennedy (D-Mass.) to introduce an equal pay bill to support defence production. Kennedy acquiesced, as did a number of other House members, but the war did not replicate either the massive production effort of World War II or the labour shortage of that era, and the bill got nowhere. Wayne Morse complained in August 1951 that the "reactionary coalition", supported by the AFL put the kibosh on the bill.

Indeed, the AFL now vehemently objected to the possibility that, through the equal pay law, the government might play a role in job evaluation or setting wage rates. Said one member of its legislative committee:

> Private property is the foundation of economic freedom. . . . It has been found desirable to keep decisions on economic matters in the hands of economic organisations, limiting the political to the formulation of objectives and basic principles. Administrative regulation of the economic order limits economic freedom and with increasing scope and degree may destroy it. . . . To attack the problem as an issue of social

justice to be cured by legislation is to perpetuate a principle based upon the assumption that women are wards of the state.

This argument seemed a bit disingenuous in view of the AFL's opposition to the ERA based on the amendment's threat to protective labour laws for women. Laws limiting women's hours of employment or barring women from certain jobs entirely certainly seemed to imply that women were wards of the state. To object to laws protecting women's rates of pay, but not those limiting their hours, lent credence to the NWP's claim that male unionists opposed the ERA for self-interested reasons rather than for the sake of women.

The NWP, itself uninterested in governmental intrusion into business matters, also continued to fight the bill's backers. The animosity between ERA supporters and equal pay advocates broke into the open again in March 1952, at a Women's Bureau conference designed to generate enthusiasm for the measure. Mildred Palmer of the National Woman's party crashed the conference and, during the question period, asked Frieda Miller why the bureau did not support the Equal Rights Amendment if it wished to expedite the matter of equal pay. With "unrestrained hatred", according to Palmer's account, Miller told her she was out of order.

Effective coalition now seemed less rather than more likely, and the situation deteriorated further when Graham Barden, the new head of the House Education and Labour Committee, made it clear he had no use for the equal pay bill. The next year, 1953, AFL president George Meany affirmed that organisation's position "We feel that in a free competitive economy, the task of establishing and safeguarding the principle as well as the practice of equal pay to women workers is properly within the province of collective bargaining and not of police action by the government." The National Association of manufacturers and the U.S. Chamber of Commerce agreed that government interference was unwarranted, and Alice paul, the founder of the National Woman's party and the nation's chief exponent of the Equal Rights Amendment, joined them: "The building up of a new, far reaching system of inspection on the question of equal pay, with power to investigate every business in the United States, administered by a colossal new government agency with vast enforcement powers, would not be helpful to women, as far as I can see."

The National Committee on Equal Pay (NCEP), which the Women's Bureau tried to resurrect after several years of inactivity, served as a clearinghouse of information. It had no power over its member organisations, many of which differed over the best strategy to pursue. Some members were frankly opposed to legislation and belonged to the group only to monitor its activities. The member organisations that were in accord with the objective of legislation all had many other time-consuming items on their agenda—including opposition to the Equal Rights Amendment, a big drain on energy and resources. Thus, the NCEP could hardly overcome the obstacles against the bill: an array of powerful organisations opposed to it, and a leadership vacuum and political inactivity on the part of the working women who presumably favoured it.

The Republicans, elected in 1952, introduced yet another wrinkle. All the proposed bills had followed Anderson's model and covered employers "affecting commerce". Republican representative Frances P. Bolton from Ohio introduced equal pay legislation in January 1954 that would amend the Fair Labour Standards Act to narrow coverage considerably from the other bids and give enforcement to the Wage and Hour Division of the Department of Labour, which had power only to mediate disputes, not to issue "case and desist" orders. By way of compromise, Bolton later submitted a different bill, which, although still modelled on the FLSA, broadened coverage a bit. To enforce the law, the secretary of labour would have to file suit.

Advocates of the original bill refused to consider Bolton's approach, unwilling to forsake coverage for any group of women workers. Bolton retreated and introduced a bill proposing "study" of the problem, while Edith Green (D-Oreg.) went to bat for the original bill. Green reintroduced the blacklist provision for guilty employers but permitted enforcement through the courts. The Department of Labour, representing the administration, insisted on the Bolton bill, and the NCEP maintained its support for the Green bill. The Women's Bureau, estranged from its traditional consistency by Leopold's appointment, also had little clout within the administration; it could influence neither side.

Meanwhile, support outside Congress was mounting. Equal pay had gone down in 1945, at a time when almost everyone agreed that women should leave the labour force. By the end of the 1950s, however, public policy had taken a new tack: concern now focused on the appropriate use of womanpower, both to fill the needs of businesses seeking white-collar workers and to meet the international challenge posed by the ostensible threat from Moscow—a challenge that highlighted the need to devote more human resources to science. In 1957 the National Manpower Council (NMC), a Columbia University panel funded by the Ford Foundation, published a landmark study entitled *Woman-power*. A comprehensive look at the experience of women in the labour force, current employment needs, and the implications of both for education, training, and public policy, the NMC analysis called women "essential" and "distinctive" workers. Attracting women to work had become a matter of national interest.

Moreover, women themselves had indicated that they intended to be a permanent part of the labour force regardless of policy incentives to stay home; now no one could accuse the government of wrecking homes by improving conditions of women's work. The sex segregation of the labour force safeguarded jobs for men, so the government could not be charged with threatening the "breadwinners", and business prosperity indicated that the nation no longer needed to fear the return of the prewar depression and job scarcity. Public opinion polls consistently supported equal pay for equal work for women.

President Eisenhower was the most prominent new

proponent of the equal pay bill. The administration had consistently favoured an equal pay law, and in 1956 Leopold persuaded Eisenhower, via the secretary of labour, to mention it in the State of the Union message. On January 5, 1956, Eisenhower told Congress: "Legislation to apply the principle of equal pay for equal work without discrimination because of sex is a matter of simple justice. I earnestly urge the Congress to move swiftly to implement these needed labour measures." Women's organisations were encouraged, and the president subsequently included equal pay recommendations in all his budget messages and four of his economic reports to Congress during the rest of his term. But the Women's Bureau did nothing else with these statements.

Important backing came from another source in 1956. Since 1947, the American Federation of Labour had opposed the equal pay bill, insisting that union membership and collective bargaining constituted a preferable route—even though in a number of unionised plants sex-segregated pay scales granted skilled women workers no higher wages than male common labourers. The Congress of Industrial Organisations, however, had steadily endorsed equal pay legislation, and when the two federations merged in 1956 the AFL-CIC adopted the CIO position, swayed by the measure's popularity: both parties had endorsed it, as had the president, and women's organisations were virtually unanimous. The AFL-CIO endorsed the Green bill, not the Bolton, and insisted on an amendment to provide for administrative enforcement by the secretary of labour. Although publicly the organisation expressed its concern that employees should not be forced to undergo the expense of legal action, the choice of administrative, rather than judicial, enforcement reflected the fear that unions would also be the target of equal pay suits. Where dual pay scales existed, some women had already sued unions, charging discrimination under collective bargaining agreements and asserting that the unions were not representing them fairly in the bargaining unit, as the law required. The labour federation assumed that the secretary of labour would give unions a more sympathetic hearing than a judge. Its anxiety over this provision meant that the group would not readily compromise on it.

The AFL-CIO position was typical of the bill's supporters: backing hinged on special considerations. There was contention even within the administration, with the Commerce department objecting to coverage broader than the FLSA and the whole notion of a separate bill. With a Republican administration in power, labour was distrustful of any suggestion of compromise, and the Republicans' business constituents, for their part, did not look kindly at the "harassment" promised by the Green bill.

Powerful enemies on the Hill, especially Graham Barden (D-N.C.), chairman of the House Education and Labour Committee, made the problems in some ways moot. Barden told Green point-blank that he considered the bill "ridiculous" and that he would never pay a woman as much as he paid his male legislative assistant. Others involved in the struggle suggested that the problem with the bill lay in the lack of hard statistical data, but that gap provided only a convenient excuse. For the last three years of the Eisenhower administration, the only significant action on equal pay legislation was the president's repeated counsel to Congress to enact it.

By the second half of the 1950s, the lack of a committed, sophisticated leadership that could gather convincing data, lobby effectively, and forge a compromise among the disparate elements backing the bill spelled defeat. The National Committee on Equal Pay served merely as an informational conduit; the administration stuck to its guns, as did the major labour organisations; and the Women's Bureau, with ties now principally to professional women rather than to its traditional constituency of labour union women and advocates for women in industry, and unwilling to alienate the Republicans' business constituency, gathered little data on the prevalence of unequal pay scales.

Like the Equal Rights Amendment, in the postwar period

equal pay legislation had suffered from the national ambivalence toward women's roles. Introduced in 1945, the legislation was overtly a tribute to women war workers, but concern for re-establishing security in the workplace for returning veterans overwhelmed the desire to achieve either that tribute or real equity for women. Throughout the fifties, as the nation restored its emotional and economic foundations within a conservative social framework, women quietly left the home during the day for the workplace, becoming an indispensable and unique part of the labour force, no longer in competition with men for jobs but filling an almost completely separated category of white-collar and service work. By the end of the decade, anxiety over working women had subsided, but equal pay proponents, fragmented by diverse goals and political beliefs and lacking effective and appropriate leadership, could not overcome the business opposition united against the bill, now its only serious obstacle. From 1945 to 1960, therefore, women received from congress virtually no recognition of their contribution to the war effort, their new place in the American economy, or their importance within the electorate. It remained for the White House to cover this political flank and do something for the women.

2

Tokens of Presidential Esteem: Women Appointees

The defeat of the Equal Rights Amendment and the failure of equal pay legislation created problems for both Republicans and Democrats in the postwar period, leaving them open to the charge that male politicians didn't care about women voters and didn't appreciate the contribution women had made toward winning the war. Women within the major parties threatened that without some recognition, faithful female party workers would simply desert their posts.

Ever since suffrage had been won in 1920, both the Republican and the Democratic parties had religiously offered something to women. After World War I, the Democrats had created the Women's Bureau, and in 1921 Congress passed legislation setting up maternal and infant health programmes. In 1922 a Republican president signed the Cable Act, which permitted American women married to foreign nationals to retain their citizenship as men did, and in 1923 Congress forbade differential pay by sex in the civil service. Both parties had created special women's divisions, and in the 1920 campaign both had adopted platform planks suggested by the newly formed League of Women Voters. As the first decade after women's suffrage wore on, however, it became clear that women, riven as they were by class interests and philosophical outlooks, were not going to form a consolidated bloc of voters, and male politicians relaxed. After that, few legislative initiatives spoke directly to women's needs, but in order not to alienate the women who were concerned about women's advancement, presidential administrations assiduously publicized the names and positions of women appointed to federal posts. Franklin Roosevelt, under the guidance of Democratic politician Molly Dewson, surpassed his predecessors by far: whereas Hoover had appointed three women to significant Senate-confirmed posts in eight years, in twelve years Roosevelt named seventeen.

In the postwar period women's organisations were divided over the Equal Rights Amendment, a reflection of the nation's general ambivalence toward equality for women. The equal pay bill was stalemated, caught in the backwash of both the ERA battle and the divisions between Republicans and Democrats, business and labour forces. Women's organisations with divergent political objectives remained united on only one point: the need to have women in policy-making positions. Appointments offered an easy way out of the policy dilemma—and the first two postwar presidents eagerly took that route.

The strategy had many advantages. "Policy-making" appointments for women evinced concern for women as voters without the ugly prospect of waging a campaign for controversial legislation or choosing sides among women's organisations. Moreover, because each president could usually work his will on the subject of appointments, it was possible to obtain this objective expeditiously. Finally, appointments represented the premier item on the agenda of the women to whom the two presidents were closest: the heads of the women's divisions of the major parties. Truman and Eisenhower each had close ties to his party's national committee, and party women considered high-level positions for deserving qualified female candidates essential. By proxy, these appointments served as encouragement and reward for the campaign work of thousands of loyal women in local precincts whose efforts were becoming more important with each election.

Women's organisations, despite their disputes over other matters, agreed unanimously on the desirability of increasing the number of women in higher government positions. Women in public office, women leaders argued, would represent women's interests, show that deserving women could attain opportunities commensurate with their abilities, offer examples to other employers that women performed admirably in responsible jobs, and make available to the nation the wisdom that educated and talented women possessed. At a June 1944 conference called by first lady Eleanor Roosevelt and held at the White House, two hundred women leaders had asked specifically that women be appointed as delegates to international conferences and as members of national policy-making bodies. Women's organisations undertook the development of rosters to ensure that "qualified" women would be visible, and Roosevelt herself continued to call attention to this demand, writing to the new president, Harry Truman, and to his associates that women's loyalty to the Democratic Party depended on these rewards.

The chairman of the Women's Division of the Democratic National Committee, Cladys Tillett, also wrote to Truman: "We should like", she reminded him, "to have women serve on all of the Peace Conferences which are to be held". She urged Truman that appointment of women to positions of power in the government would "establish the fact that the president is interested in matters pertaining to women". Truman did not, however, take much of tillett's advice. In fact, his appointment record of women in the term he served out as Franklin Roosevelt's sucessor was undistinguished: from 1945 to 1948 he appointed ony three women to important Senate-confirmed posts; Roosevel had appointed thirteen women to such posts during his first tree years in office.

But once Ewards assumed Tillett's post in 1948, the number of femie appointments jumped. Tillett had lacked effectiveness with Truman for two reasons: Truman saw her as a member of Roosevelt's team, and he felt no particular attachment to her or her proposals; and Tillett's suggestions for appointments were vague—a list of names of women she would ask the president to "consider".

Edwards, in contrast, had been a strong supporter of Truman even when FDR was president. Moreover, Edwards had pursued the course of finding a highly qualified woman for almost every available position and then making a specific pitch to the president on that candidate's behalf. She thus made it easy for Truman to fulfil her requests.

Edwards had begun her professional career as a journalist on the editorial staff of the *Chicago Tribune,* where she worked from 1918 until 1942. But when she left Chicago and moved with her husband to Washington during World War II, she gave up journalism and began to work as a volunteer at the Women's Division of the DNC. She became the division's executive secretary in 1945 and, in early 1948, its executive director. Edwards's assertive demeanour, coupled with her political know-how, elicited admiration from many of hercolleagues, although others, put off by her "unladylike" behaviour, called her a "battle-ax". Democratic party women, however, enthusiastically described her as powerful.

Edwards had been a longtime Truman backer. During the 1944 campaign she was one of the few DNC workers who always included the vice-president's name in speeches and publicity materials. In 1948, then director of the Wonen's Division, Edwards was one of the few campaign workers who thought Truman would pull off the election. In suppct she organised campaign schools for women volunteers, "Iousewives for Truman" trailers, a series of radio shows, andthe distribution of many thousands of guidebooks, fliers, platfrms, and voting records. Truman, who inherited an administation devoted to his predecessor, clearly appreciated her loyalt. When William M. Boyle, Jr., who coordinated the Truman Wistle-Stop Train, asked Edwards what she wanted as a rewardor her work, she replied: "Nothing for myself but a lot of jobs for a lot of women." From 1948 to 1952, Truman's appointment record showed a marked improvement. In addition to naming fifteen Senate-confirmed appointees, he placed two hundred more women in government.

In general, Truman had firm ties to the DNC. Robert Hannegan and J. Howard McGrath, the two-committee chairs during his first term, were longtime political associates. But his closest ties were to Edwards, whom he saw more frequently than even McGrath. In 1951 Truman offered the DNC chairmanship to Edwards—a first for woman in either party—but she declined, believing that the amount of time she would have to spend protecting herself from enemies would hinder her effectiveness.

As the head of the Women's Division, Edwards devised a procedure for getting women into appointment slots that served as a model for her successors. First she scouted among Democratic women's organisations for names of women able to hold government jobs and checked their qualifications; then she found jobs that they could fill. Before going to the president, she got the necessary clearances from party officials, senators from the nominee's state, and executive officers. After Truman made the nomination and the Senate approved it, Edwards fulfilled her share of the bargain by making sure the appointment got plenty of publicity. Women journalists, who always believed that women appointees made good copy, were willing collaborators. With regard to ambassadorships, Edwards primed Truman to appoint a woman even before a vacancy appeared. When the post of ambassador to Denmark opened, she had Eugenie Anderson ready to fill it, a special feat because Anderson was a married woman. When U.S. treasurer William A. Julian died in an accident in 1949, Edwards raced to the White House to see whether Truman would consider a woman for the position, a sinecure. When he said he would, if the woman was "qualified", Edwards came up with Georgia Neese Clark, a woman who was both a member of the DNC and a small-town banker. (Although every treasurer after Clark has been a woman, neither before nor since has the treasurer also been a banker.)

In urging Truman to accept women appointees, Edwards emphasised the political consequences of ignoring women voters. "I know there will be unfavourable reactions if not one woman is among the twenty-seven new judges", she wrote in 1949. "I hear often the criticism that most of the women's appointments are window-dressing, not on the policy level. . . . I know this is somewhat true." As a result of this particular campaign, Truman named Burnita Matthews to the district court bench.

Truman had his limits, however. For one, he intended to keep the cabinet a male preserve. He refused to consider Frances Perkins to head the Federal Security Administration because, one of his aides reported, he intended to create a Department of Welfare, and he "did not want any woman in the cabinet". He also allowed Chief Justice Fred Vinson to veto the selection of the first woman on the Supreme Court. Edwards had recommended Florence Allen, who had received her seat on the court of appeals from Franklin Roosevelt. According to aide Matthew Connelly, Truman explained: "The Justices don't want a woman. They say they couldn't sit around with their robes off and their feet up and discuss their problems." Truman also declined to appoint Florence Shientag to a vacant federal judgeship in New York, on the grounds that "her husband is already a Judge in the New York Courts and it seems to me that one Judge in the family is enough". (Shientag eventually became a judge of the family court in New York City.)

Both Edwards and leaders of women's organisations constantly reminded Truman not to forget women in appointments. The Korean War inspired a special plea for women on emergency war committees, and a new showcase body, called the Defence Advisory Committee on Women in the Services, counselled the Defence Department on the use of women in the newly integrated military services. DACOWITS, as the group was known, functioned chiefly to reassure parents (in order to support recruitment) that the government had an interest in the welfare of young women enlistees. Although enlistment of women fell far below goals, DACOWITS did accord several dozen women an ongoing role in "policy making".

The matter of women appointments did not concern the general public, however. Truman's appointments came in response to the requests of Edwards and other women lobbyists. Only a handful of letters arrived at the White House from outside Washington, and public opinion polls showed that the electorate did not want the president to turn over more power to women in government. In December 1945 a Gallup survey showed that only 26 percent of men and 38 percent of women agreed with the statement of "a woman leader" who said that "not enough of the capable women are holding important jobs in the United States Government". Furthermore, only 29 percent of men and 37 percent of women said they would vote for a woman for president even if she were the best-qualified candidate, 52 percent of men and 43 percent of women disapproved of having a "capable woman" in the cabinet, and 46 percent of men and 35 percent of women disapproved of a "capable women" on the Supreme Court. In 1947, 48 percent polled believed that women should not participate more actively in politics, and only 46 percent said they should. By 1949, 51 percent of women and 45 percent of men would have voted for a woman for president, and 48 percent of men and 60 percent of women approved President Truman's choice of a woman for minister to Luxembourg. But these data hardly represented a mandate to a president interested in appointing women in order to win votes. In fact, public support for equal pay for women was much stronger: a 1946 poll showed that 71 percent of the men and 81 percent of the women surveyed endorsed equal pay. If Truman displayed more interest in appointments than in equal pay legislation, his actions reflected the concerns of Democratic party women and the advantages of using appointments to recognise women instead of choosing a more problematic political route.

Between 1945 and 1952 Truman named eighteen women to positions requiring Senate confirmation, an average of 2.25 per year. Of these, nine were jobs women had never held before. Truman's appointments included one woman to a subcabinet position, Anna Rosenberg (assistant secretary of defence), and two ministers, Eugenie Anderson (ambassador to Demark) and Perle Mesta (minister to Luxembourg). (By way of comparison, Roosevelt, in twelve years, had appointed seventeen women, eleven of whom were "firsts".) A total of forty women (including those designated as regional comptrollers of customs and similar local officers) served during Truman's administrations in these Senate-confirmed positions (compared with thirty-seven in the Roosevelt years). In 1951–1952 women made up 2.4 percent of all executive appointments, excluding places on commissions (79 out of 3,273 posts). Edwards counting members of presidential commissions claimed that Truman had installed more than 250 women in high-level positions. Adlai Stevenson, the 1952 Democratic nominee for president, promised to follow in Truman's footsteps in his "growing reliance upon qualified women for high public posts".

Dwight Eisenhower, the Republican nominee, also understood the utility of emphasising appointments for women. He wrote to the American Association of University Women: "If it should be my destiny to serve as chief executive, I would utilise the contributions of outstanding women to the greatest extent possible. Indeed, it would be impossible to carry out the responsibilities of the office without their help." He expanded on this statement in a speech in Portland, Oregon: "I want to speak for just a second about my honest belief, my deep conviction, that we should have more women in public life." Not only, Eisenhower observed, were there two million more women than men, but women more than men worried about "the preservation and strengthening" of American values. Thus Eisenhower urged the election of women to the office of governor, and he counselled Republicans to accept women as "equal partners" in the Republican Party. Katherine Howard, the only woman on the Eisenhower Campaign Strategy Committee, pointedly brought these and similar remarks to the attention of the almost nine thousand Republican women leaders with whom she was in contact.

After Eisenhower's election in November, Republican women, following the Democratic model, moved with dispatch. Jessica Weis, director of women's activities for the Republican National Committee, promptly formulated a plan of appointments for the president's consideration. Her list of possible "top-level" positions included director of the Mint, under and assistant secretaries of the Departments of Labour, Agriculture, and Commerce, and assistant postmaster general. The position of assistant attorney general, Weis said, "has aroused more interest than any other post among women". Weis also recommended the appointment of a White House assistant at some level—"a new job for women and one which should have priority". Furthermore, Weis advised, "the United Nations is a fertile field for women's positions as so many of them are in the area of women's traditional interests", and she urged as "a matter of policy" that women be appointed to all presidential commissions. Weis also suggested that Frieda Miller be replaced as director of the Women's Bureau. Although Mary Anderson, a Democrat, had held the office during the tenure of three Republican presidents, establishing a precedent that the director not be replaced with a change in administration, Weis stated: "An early appointment would be appreciated as Miss Miller is most unpopular with Republican women." In addition to the posts Weis specified, there were, she stressed, many more at lower levels in the departments and in the judiciary. She transmitted a list of eligible women and warned that Truman had created a record Eisenhower needed to match: "We must do better."

In planning its programme for 1953, the Women's Division of the RNC asserted that women in policy-making posts, accompanied by appropriate media attention, would reap rewards for both the administration and the party. Such appointments would not only inspire women campaign workers but also win favour with the leaders of non-partisan women's groups. Indeed, in 1953 *Independent Woman* (*IW*), the magazine of the National Federation of Business and Professional Women's Clubs, featured women appointees of the Eisenhower administration in both its January and its March issues. Noting that women had been "frequently and emphatically reminded" during the campaign of the importance of their votes, the journal commented that they expected "substantial recognition" in the form of appointments to important posts. "And", *IW* stated, "the new president did make two selections that acknowledged the debt to hard campaign work on his behalf and his faith in the ability of the women chosen". *IW* highlighted the appointment of Ivy Baker Priest as treasurer, "a straight political appointment in which the honour somewhat outweighs the work involved", and of Oveta Culp Hobby as the new Federal Security administrator, and soon to be a cabinet member as the first secretary of the new Department of Health, Education, and Welfare. In March, Clare Boothe Luce, the new ambassador to Italy, appeared on *IW*'s cover, "the first woman to hold the top-ranking diplomatic post in a world power".

In the appointment of women, the Republican National Committee had a freer hand than had the DNC, because Eisenhower ran the White House differently from the way Truman had. Truman, who had a long career in politics and some involvement with political machinery, liked to be personally involved in the selection of political appointees, and he felt comfortable with the idea of patronage. The former general, in contrast, instituted a military like hierarchy, making him less accessible than Truman had been to political operatives. Moreover, with no experience in running for office, Eisenhower disdained politics and turned all but the highest-level political matters over to subordinates. Eisenhower's preference for leaving political decisions to politicians made the RNC the main clearing-house for patronage selections, and Eisenhower's willingness to depend on the committee permitted Republican women to offer suggestions on a regular basis and to have them acted upon. The RNC leadership, which sought such appointments, proved generous in granding these requests. As chairman C. Wesley Roberts explained to White House aide Sherman Adams, "The thought behind this is to try to give better recognition to women during this administration than has been done heretofore, particularly in positions of importance."

Bertha Adkins, assistant to the chairman and head of the RNC Women's Division, served as the chief conduit to Republican women and regularly enumerated Eisenhower's appointment record to the press. By July 1953 she had a list of twenty-seven women who were "playing a real role in the daily-mounting achievements of the new Administration"—proper repayment to women campaign workers who had worked "in unprecedented numbers and zeal" for Eisenhower's election. The record redounded to Adkins's credit, and she quickly became known in political circles as a powerful woman. A United Press poll named her one of the ten most influential women in Washington, because she supposedly had a "good telephone line to the White House". Adkins's reputation did not, however, reach so far as Edwards's had, and after complaints from Republican women that they were being shut out, the president began to attend publicised "breakfasts" with women party and civic leaders. *Newsweek* reported that Adkins had "ready access to President Eisenhower, who calls her by her first name and quotes her views to male politicians", a clear attempt to evoke Edwards's relationship to Truman. RNC campaign films narrated Eisenhower's achievements in appointing women to important jobs, a theme Adkins sounded repeatedly.

In April 1957 Eisenhower appointed a woman to the White House staff. In a surprise announcement to the fifteen hundred women attending the fifth annual Republican Women's Conference in Washington, he named Anne Wheaton, who had held the post of director of women's publicity of the RNC for eighteen years, as associate White House press secretary. The appointment was a public relations stroke, and the audience responded with "cheers and applause", according to newspaper accounts. Adding this one to the other slots arranged by Adkins and the RNC, Adkins claimed by 1958 that Eisenhower had appointed "more women to key posts in the Federal Government, in International Affairs and on important committees and commissions than any other Chief Executive in the Nation's history". Shortly thereafter Adkins herself assumed the position of under secretary of the Department of Health, Education, and Welfare (another "first"), thus becoming the top-ranking woman in the government.

Eisenhower's record of appointments of women did exceed Truman's. In roughly the same amount of time, Eisenhower named twenty-eight women to Senate-confirmed posts, compared to twenty for Truman. Even excluding such positions as collector of customs for localities, Eisenhower still could claim twenty-two such appointments to Truman's eighteen. Eisenhower also edged Truman out slightly in first appointments: ten for the general and nine for Truman. Each president had a woman in the cabinet; Truman, however, had not chosen Frances Perkins, a Roosevelt holdover who stayed only briefly after he took office, but Eisenhower himself selected Oveta Culp Hobby, who served until July 1, 1955. Both presidents had named one woman to the subcabinet (under and assistant secretaries), but whereas Eisenhower designated three women to serve as agency heads, Truman appointed none. Eisenhower also appointed one minister more than Truman (three to Truman's two), although Truman installed one more woman on a federal court than did Eisenhower. The Republican bested Truman's annual average of Senate-confirmed appointments by 0.5 percentage points: 2.75, up from 2.25 (84 out of 3,491 positions). With members of commissions, Eisenhower's distaff contingent numbered over four hundred. Although the actual number of women named to important positions was in fact small, it satisfied the political women who themselves took pride in their access to the chef executives. Of the three groups competing for federal attention, only the party women could claim success.

But however commendable—or unsatisfactory—the records

of Truman and Eisenhower, their appointments of women to government posts stood as a symbolic gesture more than an effective method to improve women's economic or legal position. Women's groups sought these appointments on the premise that just having women do their job properly would set an example for other employers, which in turn would expand opportunities for women at all levels. Certainly the women appointees of Harry Truman and Dwight Eisenhower, all highly qualified and competent, vindicated those who had advocated their advancement. But these appointees, as one observer noted, "did not herald a new . . . tradition in which increasing numbers of women occupied ever higher governmental positions, nor did they advance the status of women either significantly or lastingly".

Nor could they have done so. Chosen principally for their sex, not their qualifications, these women were vulnerable. India Edwards later recalled that Truman had paid her "what men have always considered the ultimate compliment to a female: that I operated like a man". In the absence of a movement for women's rights, when "operating like a man" was the standard of excellence, no woman in an important governmental job could become the champion of the women's cause without calling her legitimacy into question—unless that position dealt exclusively with women's issues.

Mary Anderson, director of the Women's Bureau, which was under the aegis of the secretary of labour, encountered this problem with regard to Frances Perkins. Anderson wrote:

> When Frances Perkins came in as Secretary of Labour, we were all jubilant, because we thought that at last we would have someone who really understood our problems and what we were up against and who would fight for us. . . . But it did not turn out to be that way. . . . The terrible publicity she was subjected to because she was the first woman cabinet officer was a great handicap. . . . It was especially discouraging to me to find that the Women's Bureau was not of great interest to her though I understood that she was preoccupied with other things and did not want to be thought of as a woman who was too closely identified with women's problems.

Perkins, herself in part a token, understood the difficulties common to token appointees. Often highly qualified, but selected because of their sex or because they possess a specific visible racial, ethnic, or physical characteristic essentially irrelevant to the execution of their job—selected, that is, for the specific political purpose of recognising the group they represent—token appointees are expected to ignore in the fulfilment of their duties the very attribute for which they were chosen. Tokens have the responsibility of proving that the trait that identifies them does not in act constitute a handicap. They thus labour under the burden that their mistakes impugn not only their own abilities, but those of all members of their group as well. Conversely, of course, the successes of "token" appointees do both confirm their abilities and confer at least a modicum of status on the group they represent.

But the postwar experience of the pursuit of token appointments for women reveals the drawback of this strategy. By diverting attention from policy questions, a roster of token appointments made in response to requests from an interested group allowed the presidents to duck thorny political problems without serious reprisals and to evade the debate over more significant issues. Convinced of the value of female appointments for both women and their parties, and concerned with the publicity deriving from the appointments rather than with policy goals, the party women who nominated the candidates did so in general without regard to the views of the designee on specific matters of interest to women activists. The appointees for the most part had no policy role with respect to women's issues.

Both Truman and Eisenhower met their obligations to their female constituents in a way that was ultimately cosmetic, without addressing more fundamental questions regarding the position of women in America. Because token appointments represented a traditional means of recognising groups excluded from real power, the political system yielded willingly to the requests of party women. The ease with which the appointments were obtained signalled the limits of appointees' ability to alter the status of the group they personified: if these appointments had been of greater consequence, they would have been harder to come by. Moreover, the benefits of the appointment practice did not filter down to the women who were not direct recipients of presidential largesse.

During World War II, American women had proven themselves heroines on the home front; afterwards, they quietly took up again the responsibility to re-establish secure and stable homes. By 1960, a supposedly grateful nation had left them without any legislative or executive protection from discrimination, as vulnerable to arbitrary treatment in the public and private sectors as ever they had been before.

3

A New Frontier for Women: The Kennedy Administration

The inauguration of John Kennedy in January 1961 marked a sea change: the end of postwar politics in America. For some fifteen years, national leadership had dealt with postwar problems: the establishment of a sound national and international economy; rebuilding Europe's industrial base; ensuring jobs for breadwinners in the United States; capping inflation and ending wartime government regulation; and coping with newly organised international spheres of influence. With the nation looking over its shoulder at two decades of depression and war, both Truman and Eisenhower had confronted the task of re-establishing a stable society. Now the time had come to face the future.

Elected in 1952, the avuncular Eisenhower had presided over eight years of national consolidation; but if Eisenhower's relaxed demeanour had suited the temper of the electorate in the fifties, by 1960 problems had emerged that called for a more active approach. The GI bill, with its subsidised mortgages for veterans, and a national highway construction programme had permitted young couples to leave the crowded cities and buy homes in the suburbs in which to raise their families; they commuted to work by private car. The cities they had left, however, were now disproportionately populated by the poor, who were stuck in decaying and depressing tenements. Although personal income had jumped in the decade, in 1957 a severe recession signalled an end to the feeling of national prosperity. That same year the Soviet Union further undermined national confidence by orbiting two space satellites, feats that appeared to indicate a significant advantage in technical capabilities. Other observers indicted the complacency and boredom afflicting middle-class Americans. During the last two years of Eisenhower's administration, the overwhelmingly democratic Congress confronted an unyielding chief executive. By the time the 1960 campaign began, John Kennedy's clear liberal theme—his exhortation to "get the country moving again"—resonated strongly for many Americans. His election expressed a readiness on the part of a large segment of the population to meet the challenges of the 1960s head on.

A nascent liberalism had been visible even during the 1950s. The Supreme Court had ordered the desegregation of the nation's public schools in 1954, thus fuelling the civil rights movement. The Democrats had firmly regained control of Congress, although the presidency stayed in Republican hands. By 1959 several liberal Democrats—among them Kennedy, Edmund Muskie, Eugene McCarthy, Frank Church, and Philip Hart—and liberal Republicans—Nelson Rockefeller, Mark Hatfield, Clifford Case—had won election in either congressional races or gubernatorial contests. A small antinuclear movement sought the control of atomic weapons.

Despite his victory, the narrow margin by which Kennedy won—two-tenths of 1 percent—hampered his efforts to enact the multifaceted programme he detailed under the rubric "The New Frontier" in his nomination acceptance speech. As the days of the new administration slipped by, the Kennedy "style" occupied more newspaper space than the Kennedy accomplishments. Indeed, his administration terminated so abruptly that many nave since claimed that the Kennedy administration was mostly style and that, if his foreign affairs decisions were misbegotten and dangerous, his domestic efforts had hardly any substance at all.

But style and substance are not unrelated phenomena. Kennedy's call to public concern—"Ask not what your country can do for you, ask what you can do for your country"—represented a new dedication to an aggressive liberal politics, and it served as a national inspiration. After the election Michael Walzer, writing in the left-liberal periodical *Dissent,* observed: "There is an openness to new ideas probably unlike anything since the thirties." In March 1961 a *New York Times* reporter described the change in the White House: "In two short months President Kennedy has set for the White House a physical and mental pace unmatched in modern times . . . in an urgent effort to solve or alleviate accumulated domestic and foreign problems." Seven major pieces of legislation had been sent to Congress: aid to depressed areas, extension of unemployment benefits, a 25 percent increase in the minimum wage, medical care for the aged, federal aid to education, urban renewal, and commodity control programmes. The development of the Peace Corps, Kennedy's sympathy with Martin Luther King, his public appreciation of the arts reverberated with the young. Even many of those who did not join the Peace Corps or engage in voter registration drives in black communities felt imbued with a sense of possibility and the expectation that Americans would do more and become better—that problems existed to be solved, not endured, that poverty, racism, war, Communism, illiteracy, hunger, and ugliness could and therefore should be eliminated by national dedication to a public purpose.

It was a legacy that had both good results and bad. Most of the domestic legislation that Lyndon Johnson succeeded in getting through Congress in the terrible aftermath of Kennedy's assassination had already been initiated by the Kennedy team. So had the extended war in Vietnam. But in both cases the "style" was an authentic political event. It encouraged national energies that continued beyond Kennedy's life, through the 1960s, facilitating movements for women's rights, consumers' rights, ecology, and mental health services. It also produced, in the words of historians David Burner and Thomas West, "some of the finest social legislation . . . of the century".

Kennedy's style inspired Americans who saw him only from a distance or through the cool medium of television, but his impact on his own team was even more intense. During the transition, Kennedy's staff drew up extensive programmes for each department, and his appointees all recognised that the first time in years proposals for federal action were welcome.

It was characteristic of Kennedy's pragmatic liberalism, however, that the proposals sought not the ideal but the feasible. His liberalism lacked the fervour of Eleanor Roosevelt's and Adlai Stevenson's, and Kennedy distrusted fanaticism. Respectful of intellectuals but impatient with excessive deliberation, he favoured "technical" solutions over ideological ones. Thus, aware of his razor-thin electoral victory, and preferring movement to inertia, Kennedy often chose executive action when it was a possibility. This strategy allowed him to avoid confrontation with an unintimidated Congress, whose Republican—Southern Deocratic majority stood able to turn back any Kennedy initiative, especially in civil rights.

So, in response to a burgeoning civil rights movement, the Justice Department under Attorney General Robert Kennedy brought suits to protect black voting rights, and Kennedy appointed blacks to executive positions to compensate further for the lack of legislation. He also appointed a committee on equal employment opportunity to replace two existing but ineffective committees. The order banning discrimination in housing came in November 1962, and in June 1963, only two and a half years into his term, Kennedy told the nation that his administration had aligned itself with a civil rights revolution. As white-run governments in the South responded with violence to black demands for decent treatment, the Kennedy administration employed conciliation, exhortation, political pressure, litigation, and ultimately federal troops to persuade racist opponents to obey the law. In 1963, after a review of federal government and federal contractor employment practices, the administration introduced an omnibus civil rights bill to mandate equality in employment and public accommodations. John and Robert Kennedy did not keep all their promises to black civil rights leaders, and often the administration's dilatory responses indicated grudging acceptance of political realities rather than a spontaneous sense of moral outrage. Still, the Kennedy administration offered more support to black activists than any previous administration, and many black Americans regarded the Kennedy brothers as heroes.

If Congress viewed the civil rights measures with mixed emotions, they welcomed Kennedy's proposals concerning the economy. When Kennedy took office, 7 percent of the labour force was looking for jobs. Even with the sometimes controlling influence of conservative Southern Democrats, Kennedy succeeded in extending Social Security benefits, raising the minimum wage, and procuring federal monies for housing and public works. Economic bills had two purposes: to revitalise the economy and lift poor Americans out of poverty, and to exploit national human resources in order to achieve a stronger position with respect to the Soviet Union. Expanding opportunities for women would further both those goals.

Democratic Party Women on the Outs

Kennedy started with no particular public agenda for women. Like most other male politicians, he was aware that women voted, but in the absence of a broad based movement for women's rights he did not devote much attention to winning their votes as a bloc. As always, his mother and sisters figured prominently in his campaign, and, although he did not seek out women as advisers, he had accepted the assistance of Marjorle Lawson, a prominent black attorney, in his 1958 senatorial race. In 1960 she became director of the civil rights section of the presidential campaign. Congresswoman Edith Green ran Kennedy's campaign in Oregon. Few top political party women played a role in Kennedy's presidential campaign, because few had joined him for the primary battles. After he won the nomination, the reception from the Kennedy campaign was lukewarm for most of the women who had supported his opponents. (Despite Kennedy's overtures, Eleanor Roosevelt chose to keep her distance.)

Margaret Price of Michigan, a close associate of Michigan governor G. Mennen Williams, represented virtually the only Democratic committeewoman who had any clout within the Kennedy camp. The Michigan Democratic party had identified itself with the Kennedy's early in the campaign and had offered effective assistance. Williams himself recommended that Price, whom many Democrats regarded as the most competent woman politician in the country, become art of the Kennedy entourage. Price worked closely at the Democratic convention with Kennedy's aide Myer Feldman. After his nomination the candidate rewarded Price for her efforts by giving her the Democratic National Committee position held by Katie Louchheim, vice-chairman of the DNC and director of women's activities. (Incensed at being shunted aside, Louchheim nevertheless accepted a minor post at the State Department.)

From that position Price tried to influence the candidate with regard to women's issues. In a campaign memorandum, Price counselled that "women (particularly organisation and leadership women) respond to being 'included in'". Price promised that if Kennedy offered evidence that qualified women were welcome, he would gain "enormously" in respect and allegiance from women community leaders. At the moment, she observed, "the absence of professional women in any staff capacity in the Kennedy entourage has led to an initial impression that his is an all-male cast". The presence of women would "give an incentive" to women throughout party ranks, she said. Price recommended that Kennedy present her to the press to emphasise the importance of women in policy-making roles and urged him to hire more women "onto his inner circle". Moreover, she advised, women party leaders needed to be integrated into the campaign and invited to party conferences, which at the moment were all male.

But Kennedy preferred his largely male coterie, and he ignored her recommendations. He also declined to give Price a visible role in the campaign. Instead of including her in the group that travelled with the candidate, campaign manager Robert Kennedy recommended that Price go on independent campaign trips. She objected, saying that party leaders disliked making the additional arrangements. Kennedy refused to acquiesce; of the more than five hundred campaign stops Kennedy made, Price appeared with him on only twenty-one occasions.

After he won the party nomination Kennedy did make an increased effort to attract the women's vote, but not by wooing party women or promising stepped-up efforts to improve women's status. The campaign formed two committees: the Committee of Labour Women, which included such notable reformers as Mary Anderson, Elizabeth Christman, Gladys Dickason, and others and was run by Esther Peterson of the Industrial Union Division of the AFL-CIO, and the Women's Committee for New Frontiers, which also boasted prominent liberal women, including Frances Perkins, Eleanor Roosevelt, Eugenie Anderson, Anna Rosenberg, and Agnes Meyer. These committees served in publicity and fund raising not policy: they were intended to indicate the candidate's sympathy for the causes for which these women were known. Thus, they made special efforts to call women's attention to programmes regarding medical care for the aged, federal aid to education, and full employment, issues that Kennedy's staff believed concerned female voters.

On only a few occasions did Kennedy address proposals aimed specifically at the position of women. He hinted at one female appointment, saying that a consumer counsel in the Office of the President would be "perhaps a woman familiar with consumer problems". In a letter to daycare advocate Elinor Guggenheimer, a member of the Women's Committee for New Frontiers, he endorsed federal aid for childcare. Finally, to the surprise of many, including members of his own staff, he also appeared to have signed a letter endorsing the Equal Rights Amendment, which he had never before supported; although this statement turned out to have been a campaign blunder, it remained the official stance. (This incident is discussed in full in chapter 5). The Republican candidate, Richard Nixon, paid hardly more attention to the status of women; his promises tended to concentrate on appointing women to top-level positions, but his endorsement of the ERA was genuine, in keeping with Republican tradition.

After Kennedy's hairbreadth victory, Price, following her predecessors, encouraged the president to include women in his administration. In a transition memorandum she maintained that, although "women should not be appointed to high public positions simply because they are women, . . . pressures are strong for the appointment of women to top level public office. Millions of citizens . . . with give close attention to these appointments and the serious waste of manpower that would result if such appointments are not made". Price recommended that the new president appoint women to posts not previously held by women and briefly reviewed for him the records of Presidents Wilson, Roosevelt, Truman, and Eisenhower. She then enumerated, department by department, the jobs in which she thought a woman could appropriately serve: secretary of labour, ambassador, delegate to the United Nations, assistant secretaries of the Treasury, defence, and labour, treasurer, and director of the Mint. Unlike Edwards, Price did not fight for specific women to fill specific positions; instead, she attached to her memorandum the resumes of some two dozen women. Of this group, only four eventually received Senate-confirmed appointments: Esther Peterson, as assistant secretary of labour and director of the Women's Bureau; Eugenie Anderson, as minister to Bulgaria; Elizabeth Smith, as treasurer of the United States; and Lucia Cormier, as collector of customs for Portland, Maine. Of these, Peterson would clearly have gotten her position without Price's efforts; treasurer had been a "woman's job" since

Harry Truman named Georgia Neese Clark to the post; Anderson had first been appointed an ambassador in 1949; and collector of customs of Portland, Maine, was a position of no policy-making significance. Twelve other women received minor or temporary appointments. Price, who had also vainly sought an administration job, was disappointed in the small numbers.

Displeased party women attacked Kennedy on Price's behalf as well as their own. After Kennedy selected his cabinet, Doris Fleeson, a well-known journalist, commented scornfully in her column: "At this stage, it appears that for women the New Frontiers are the old frontiers." A month after the inauguration, Emma Guffey Miller told Kennedy: "It is a grievous disappointment to the women leaders and ardent workers that so few women have been named to worthwile positions. . . . As a woman of long political experience, I feel the situation has become serious and I hope whoever is responsible for it may be made to realise that the result may well be disastrous." A reply came not from the president himself, but from presidential aide Lawrence O'Brien, which offended Miller further. Such thing, Miller complained, "never would have happened under Frankline D. Roosevelt or President Truman". When the list of the fourteen top assistants to Peace Corps director Sargent Shriver included not a single female name, Fleeson again lambasted the President, declaring it "ludicrous" that of two hundred appointments he had made so far, only eight had gone to women. Even Eisenhower, wrote Fleeson, had done better than that.

Margaret Price loyally tried to redeem the Kennedy appointment record. On November 1, 1961, she published a list of the eighty-eight women named to administration posts, but, rather than helping, the enumeration merely called attention to the problem. Of that number, fifty-four had received appointments to minor committees and commissions or to positions such as collector of customs, fourteen became special assistants to executives (probably named by other government officials, not by the president), and eight of the others were simply reappointed to jobs such as emergency planning office directors or representatives to various United Nations bodies. Only a few held positions of real visibility or had the ability to make policy: Anderson, Peterson, White House physician Dr. Janet Travel, Frances Willis as ambassador to Ceylon, and Marie MeGuire as commissioner of the Public Housing Administration. Esther Peterson was the only woman in the subcabinet. Genevieve Blatt, secretary of the Pennsylvania Democratic State Committee, wrote to Emma Guffey Miller a month after the list came out: "Things do seem to get worse and worse, so far as women in Washington are concerned, don't they?"

In July 1963 one man did seem finally to get the President's attention. Clayton Fritchey, former publicity director of the Democratic National Committee, serving the Kennedy administration at the United States mission to the United Nations, put his thought in writing at the president's request. Fritchey began by reminding the president of the growing numbers of women voters and the fact that in many suburbs the women were "virtually running local politics". Fritchey cautioned against thinking that these women failed to notice female appointments. "Consciously, or not", he argued, "women naturally seize on any evidence that tends to dispel the age-old image of an inferior sex", which accounted, said Fritchey, for Eleanor Roosevelt's popularity and influence. With Roosevelt gone (she had died in 1962), the administration lacked any "notable" or "really famous" women, like Anna Rosenberg, Frances Perkins, India Edwards, or Oveta Culp Hobby, in its service. Happily, Fritchey remarked, it would take fairly few appointments "to create a favourable new impression". Fritchey recommended the appointment of an assistant attorney general ("the woods are full of capable women lawyers"), either a White House special assistant or an assistant secretary of commerce specialising in consumer affairs, another women ambassador, and a new secretary of Health, Education, and Welfare, "the ideal post". Appointment of an "outstanding Negro woman" would help as well. Such a programme would guarantee the president favourable publicity—politically, it was a case of "everything to gain and nothing to lose", according to Fritchey. In addition, such a strategy was equitable. He urged speedy action "to avoid the appearance of political motivation". Although he had personally solicited Fritchey's memorandum, Kennedy ignored the advice. He also disregarded the counsel of Emanuel Celler, the powerful chairman of the House Judiciary Committee. Celler, who abhorred the Equal Rights Amendment, considered appointments an appropriate way to elevate the status of women, and he had written twice to chide the president for failing to name women to the bench.

The Kennedy record of appointments that provoked these complaints did compare unfavourably with that of his predecessors, but not overmuch. Kennedy made only ten Senate-confirmed appointments of women to policy-making executive and judicial posts, where in a comparable period Truman, who won extravagant praise for his record, had made fifteen, and Eisenhower fourteen. No president, Kennedy included, utilised the talents of women significantly. Women held 2.4 percent of all executive positions in the Kennedy administration, the same percentage they had held under the two previous presidents.

But the problem was more than mere numbers. Kennedy also neglected visible appointments, becoming, moreover, the first president since Herbert Hoover never to have had a woman in his cabinet. He also appointed fewer "first women" to positions formerly held exclusively by men, thus forfeiting the good publicity that kind of nomination always received. Kennedy's admirers had anticipated that he would exceed the performance of his predecessors; their expectations were unmet, and they responded with vocal protests.

But the displeasure Kennedy elicited came more from his neglect of women party leaders than from his record. These leaders had expected to control appointments of women, as they had in the Roosevelt and Truman years. Thwarted, they resented both their loss of influence and their lack of access to the president. India Edwards remarked that, with the Kennedy administration, "there was no one at the DNC . . . who had any influence . . . when it came to women's affairs". Emma Guffey Miller voiced dismay over the exclusion of Price from White House inner circles: The administration has been lax in recognising Democratic women. . . . In the Roosevelt and Truman Administrations, the Vice Chairman [and head of women's affairs] was always consulted when women were being named to important posts, but now all Margaret Price knows is what she sees in the newspapers. This is not going to help the party.

Indeed, the White House appointment procedures excluded Price, as Kennedy broke away from past methods of operation and instituted an ongoing, systematic talent hunt for "the best and the brightest". "Kennedy", wrote Thedore Sorensen, "wanted a ministry of talent". Both before the inauguration and after, the Kennedy search for people to staff his administration claimed to ignore considerations of campaign contributions or political benefits in favour of ability. The president would not, Sorensen boasted, "name a woman or a Negro to the Cabinet merely for the sake of show". A decision to seek excellence did not, of course, automatically exclude women (or blacks); clearly, women (and blacks) could be found among the "best and brightest" minds in the nation. Yet the process Kennedy created to find his appointees not only omitted Margaret Price and insulted Democratic Party women, but it also actually worked against potential women nominees.

Because the Kennedy staff conducted the search from the White House, women lost the use of traditional procedures which had been sensitive to the political utility of women party workers, and which had included a well-established role for them to play in appointments. Except for minor patronage positions, the White House paid no attention whatever to the DNC, figuring that it would not be a source of likely candidates, male or female, and suggestions sent by Congress members, too, were usually discarded. Dan Fenn, who headed the talent search, observed: "It is a rare guy who comes up through a party or campaign organisation who can be Assistant Secretary of Defence for Procurement. This view represented a departure from the position of earlier administrations, which, often filled such posts with party faithful. The talent search Fenn conducted instituted no compensatory method of including women; Fenn said he experienced no pressure at all to pay special attention to the appointment of women, evidence that Price was not playing her traditional role.

Women, moreover, were not likely to be found in the places the Kennedy staff did look. The search centred on elite universities, boards and executive's suites of major corporations, and presitigious law firms, where women were few in number. This effective reduction of the pool of acceptable women candidates made their selection proportionately less likely. The blatant discrimination that kept women out of high-level jobs did not have to come from the Kennedy team; it had already taken place.

The Kennedy team shared a bias against women, to be sure. A memorandum from Dan Fenn concerning the post of commissioner of education listed Mary Bunting, the president of Radcliffe College, as eighth choice, citing as handicaps both her lack of public education experience and her sex. Fenn would later explain that he had viewed her gender as a drawback because of a "silly social assumption", which he shared, that women were less likely to have managerial talent and staff would be unhappy to work under a female supervisor.

It was improbable, however, that Kennedy was more prejudiced than Truman or Eisenhower had been. Kennedy's appointment of Janet Travell as his personal physician and the testimony of Esther Peterson, whom he named assistant secretary of labour, Representative Edith Green, who managed his campaign in Oregon, and Senator Maurine Neuberger (D-Oreg.) argue against the premise put forth by some writers that the reason Kennedy did not appoint women was that he categorically disliked working with them and failed to respect their ability or judgement. Bill Lawrence, a journalist who had been president of the National Press Club, complained that Kennedy pressured him repeatedly to get the club to admit women journalists as members, a change Lawrence opposed. More plausibly it was the Kennedy search method, rather than an overt Kennedy intention, that excluded women more completely than in previous administrations.

Nothing impelled Kennedy to adopt a strategy of recognising women voters through appointments. His association with the DNC, which emphasised political patronage, differed from that of former presidents and their national committees. Kennedy's political organisation had been largely an independent creation, based on developing contacts in local areas and run by close personal associates. With no particular attachment to the DNC, he had little reason to rely on its officers for counsel. In fact, the power of both national committees had begun generally to decline as primaries and television advertising assumed an ever greater role in candidate selection. In addition, Margaret Price was herself deferential, unwilling to press her views on Kennedy or threaten retaliation for being overlooked. (When Kennedy, for example, declined to address the biennial Campaign Conference for Democratic Women, a gathering of more than three thousand, Price accepted the decision; only when India Edwards wrote to the president threatening to cancel the meeting did Kennedy capitulate.) But also, as a member of the reform wing of the Democratic party in Michigan, Price felt little commitment to the Democratic party in Michigan, Price felt little commitment to the patronage aspect of party politics. Viewing herself less as an advocate for women within the Democratic party than an advocate among women for the Democratic party, she did not work as hard for women's appointments as Edwards had. "The surest way for a group to shut itself out of the appointment process is for it to blunder into a strategy of reticence", one political scientist has observed—which is just what Price unwittingly did.

But appointments for women fell by the wayside primarily

because Kennedy preferred another route: the fulfilment of the agenda of the Women's Bureau coalition of women's liberal and labour organisations, a course charted by Women's Bureau director Esther Peterson. The implementation of the Women's Bureau programme constituted a New Frontier for women. Unlike token appointments, the new plan directly addressed the problem of women's status in American society, and its impact was far-reaching.

Women's Bureau Ascendancy

Throughout the fifteen-year struggle over equal legislation and the Equal Rights Amendment, the members of the Women's Bureau coalition had looked to the bureau to provide, in the words of the second bureau director Frieda Miller, both "factual information and leadership". In general, the "leadership" the bureau provided was disappointing. Although the bureau accepted the mandate, and although it saw itself as the bulwark against "extremist feminist" organisations that promoted the "so-called Equal Rights Amendment", none of the bureau's first three directors had been in a position to provide effective direction to the bureau's supporters. In 1961 the situation finally changed. During the Kennedy administration, thanks to the president's interest in an activist programme and his reliance on the team in the Labour Department, the Women's Bureau at last assumed the role it had claimed for the previous decades.

Directors of the women's bureau had always been low-level appointees. Mary Anderson, the bureau's first chief, received her position from a Democratic president and then served three Republican presidents; none sought her advice. In Franklin Roosevelt's administration, Anderson was far outclassed by Eleanor Roosevelt, Molly Dewson, and Frances Perkins. As secretary of labour, Perkins downplayed women's issues in order to minimise her own vulnerability, and the Great Depression made special claims for women inopportune with so many male "breadwinners" out of work. Anderson played a small role within the Roosevelt administration.

Frieda Miller had come to the Women's Bureau in 1944 from the post of industrial commissioner for the state of New York, a job she had had since 1938. Her background included little lobbying experience. Although she had been executive secretary of the Philadelphia Women's Trade Union League in the early twenties and a factory inspector for the International Ladies Garment Workers' Union before becoming the head of the Women in Industry Division of New York State in 1929, she also had no influence with labour unions. Once in federal office, Miller indulged her predilection for the international aspects of the bureau's work, including extensive participation in the activities of the International Labour Organisation. Because she was interested in maintaining peace, she restrained assertive behaviour on the part of the bureau's advisory committees, comprising women's organisations and labour union groups. Truman, on record as favouring the Equal Rights Amendment but unwilling to alienate labour groups, relied on appointments of women to let him steer clear of the dispute. He had little to say to Miller, and her role of policy maker within the Truman administration was minor.

Alice Leopold's problems were even more acute than Miller's, whom she succeeded in 1953. Leopold, too, had been a state executive (secretary of the state of Connecticut), but unlike Miller she had had few connections to working-class women or their middle-class protectors. When Leopold took over, she saw no need to convene the bureau's advisory groups on a regular basis, and so communications with the Women's Bureau coalition members became sporadic and formal. In addition, her apparent willingness to soften the bureau's anti-ERA stance made the coalition distrustful of her motives, with many inside and outside the bureau believing that Leopold's primary interest concerned professional women rather than the lower-paid working women the bureau had traditionally championed. Leopold could hardly function as a good leader of the Women's Bureau coalition, or serve as an effective liaison among the various groups supporting equal pay legislation. In 1954 Labour

Secretary James P. Mitchell alienated women's organisations further when he "promoted" Leopold nominally to be his special assistant for "Women's Affairs", because the Republicans linked the change to a suggestion that the Women's Bureau, the symbol and vehicle of the protection of women, be abolished.

The Kennedy administration took a different tack, elevating the position of Women's Bureau director and granting her a genuine role in policy making—a departure having its roots in the Kennedy administration's affinity for its labour constituency. Kennedy's liberalism had found its most consistent expression in relationship to labour issues. While he was a member of the House, representing a working-class district of Boston, his voting record on bills of interest to labour had been virtually perfect: 100 percent for four of the six years, 90 percent and 88 percent in the remaining two. As a member of the House Labour Committee, Kennedy had also taken an active part in opposing the Taft-Hartley Act, an unusual step for a first-term congressman. Although he butted heads with some union leaders for refusing to oppose all reforms, he spoke effectively in favour of the union shop, industry-wide bargaining, and the right to strike. Unable to get Taft-Hartley modified, he voted against the final bill and supported President Truman's unsuccessful veto of it.

In the Senate, where his ties to a working-class constituency were looser, Kennedy continued to display commitment to rank-and-file workers as well as to the concerns of union leaders, winning respect even when he took an opposing view. As chair of the Senate Subcommittee on Labour, Kennedy deftly conducted hearings on a bill to extend minimum wage coverage, confronting Eisenhower's labour secretary, James Mitchell, and publicly forging an alliance with George Meany on the issue. In March 1958 Kennedy played a crucial role in enabling Walter Reuther, the president of the United Auto Workers, to testify before the McClellan Committee investigating corruption in labour unions ("labour rackets"); in response, Reuther labelled him "a real saint towards the UAW". Kennedy won still more publicity as the author of legislation to reform the practices that the rackets committee had uncovered, a strategy Meany opposed and tried to head off by instituting internal policing procedures. When Kennedy insisted on going through with a bill to require labour unions to disclose their finances. Meany publicly rebuked him. Both agreed to negotiate their differences privately, and Meany subsequently lauded Kennedy's openness to and respect for opposing arguments. Kennedy included the recommendations of AFL-CIO special counsel Arthur Goldberg in the next version of the bill, and the relationship between the senator and his labour constituents prospered. At the opening of the 1960 Democratic presidential convention, Communications Workers chief Joseph A. Beirne told a reporter that a majority of the AFL-CIO union heads favoured Kennedy. After Kennedy's nomination, organised labour pursued its customarily vigorous support for the Democratic candidate in a presidential election.

Kennedy named Arthur Goldberg secretary of labour, and Goldberg almost immediately assumed a unique role in the administration. One of the stars of the cabinet, Goldberg impressed Kennedy with his intellect and his professional competence. Goldberg had joined the Kennedy campaign early, so the president had no doubt of his loyalty, and he consulted him on a wide range of domestic policy issues. Moreover, Coldberg surrounded himself with extremely capable associates; AFL-CIO people filled out his staff, and Goldberg worked hard to maintain not only his fine reputation at the White House but also his close connection to George Meany. In august 1962 Meany commented that at no time had there been closer cooperation between the labour movement and the administration in power.

As part of that alliance, John Kennedy named Esther Peterson director of the Women's Bureau. A native of Provo, Utah, raised in a Republican Mormon family, Peterson had been introduced to the labour movement at Columbia University in 1929, when she enrolled at Teachers College for graduate training after receiving a bachelor's degree in physical education from

Brigham Young University. During the 1930s she taught in schools for workers, including the Bryn Mawr Summer School for Women Workers in Industry, and helped to organise teachers' unions in Massachusetts. In 1939 she joined the Amalgamated Clothing Workers Union (ACW) as assistant director for education under the wing of ACW sent her to Washington as its legislative representative. As a labour lobbyist, she participated in the National Committee on Equal Pay, the National Committee on the Status of Women, and the Labour Advisory Council of the Women's Bureau. She also initiated her association with labour lawyer Arthur Goldberg and John Kennedy in 1947 a freshman representative from Massachusetts, whom she was assigned to lobby. In 1948 she went abroad with her husband, Oliver Peterson, a labour attaché in the Foreign Service, and spent the next decade participating in the international union movement in Sweden and Belgium. When she returned to the United States in 1957, Peterson became a legislative representative in the Industrial Union department of the AFL-CIO, which Arthur Goldberg served as special counsel, and she resumed her professional relationship with Kennedy, now a senator and a member of the Senate Labour and Public Welfare Committee. Peterson had a reputation as a consummate lobbyist; she in turn admired Kennedy's willingness to ask questions and his ability to absorb answers and approach issues in new ways. Following labour's position, while in the Senate John Kennedy supported equal pay legislation and refused to endorse the Equal Rights Amendment, citing the hazard to protective labour laws.

Peterson joined Kennedy's campaign as soon as he announced his intention to run for the presidency. Robert Kennedy, the candidate's brother and campaign manager, offered Peterson a full-time campaign staff job organising labour support, but Peterson declined because family illness restricted her freedom to travel. She continued to supply advice in an informal way, however, and at the convention she worked with Kennedy forces to swing her home state of Utah into the

Kennedy column. Immediately after the convention, Peterson began to work with Arthur Goldberg at the campaign headquarters under Lawrence O'Brien and Ralph Dungan, making sure that Kennedy acknowledged labour at every turn.

After the election, Ralph Dungan asked her what position she wanted. Because of her interest in working women, and because the National Consumers League had asked her to, Peterson chose the Women's Bureau. Peterson's appointment had the support of virtually every member of the Women's Bureau coalition. Mary Anderson, the bureau's first director and the founder of the National Committee on Equal Pay, sent the president-elect a letter, signed by fourteen other women representing major women's organisations, seeking Peterson's selection; the letter argued that under Peterson's direction "the true purposes of the Bureau" would be realised. Louise Stitt, chairman of the board of the National Consumers League (NCL), started a letter-writing campaign on behalf of Peterson, an NCL board member. With the backing, and that of the labour unions (she was the only woman on George Meany's list of desirable nominees), her selection was assured, even though the BPW, not a traditional member of the Women's Bureau coalition, preferred a different candidate. Moreover, Goldberg saw to it that Peterson got more than the directorship of a minor bureau; within eight months, Congress created a new assistant secretary position for Peterson to hold with the Women's Bureau post. With her assumption of that position, Peterson became the highest-ranking woman in the Kennedy administration.

The assistant secretary post had the "growing role of women in the work force of the nation" as its particular purview, anticipating that the number of women workers would be likely to grow twice as fast as that of male workers. As assistant secretary, Peterson had charge of the Bureau of Labour Standards, the Bureau of Employees' Compensation, and the Employees' Compensation Appeal Board. Her responsibilities therefore included policy decisions concerning male as well as female workers. With more actual authority than any previous bureau director, she was able to provide to the Women's Bureau coalition effective leadership unprecedented in the history of the bureau's existence. The bureau took as its domain twenty-four million working women—a third of all American women—concentrated in clerical, service, and factory work. More than half of them were married, and one in four had children; on average they earned 60 percent what male workers did. When she came to office in 1961, Peterson did not create a new agenda—she simply sought the implementation of the programme that labour women had long supported: equal pay legislation and a national commission on women.

With her programme and her resources, Peterson eclipsed Margaret Price and her proposals for the appointment of women. DNC member Emma Guffey Miller, who also resented Peterson's opposition to the ERA, viewed the situation with utter disgust. Writing to congratulate Katie Louchheim on her new position at the Department of State (to a slightly less trivial post than she had received at the beginning of the administration), Miller said: "We women are very proud of you and wish the President would name more women to important positions, especially women who are for women instead of the Esther Peterson type as she goes out of her way to do the contrary thing."

The Kennedy years marked the transition from a procedure of marginal utility for women—token appointments—to one that addressed women's social and economic position more directly. Kennedy neglected appointments of women, but he was protected from charges of indifference by the establishment of the President's Commission on the Status of Women and administration pursuit of equal pay legislation. On the forty-second anniversary of the suffrage amendment, August 26, 1962, Peterson warned that the Republicans were "planning to take a crack at the Administration" for the dearth of women appointees. She was unperturbed, however, and assured the White House that the interim report of the new commission "would draw the fangs of any such attack". The British publication *The*

Economist, which commended Kennedy for his creation of the commission, accurately observed that "many women felt that Mr. Kennedy could have supported their cause more vigorously by appointing a woman to his cabinet as his recent predecessors had done." But Peterson was essentially correct. Following her advice, Kennedy got credit for a substantial record on women's issues. Moreover, the programme Peterson laid out for him had greater potential to affect the lives of American women than had all the female appointments of the previous fifteen years.

4

The Equal Pay Act of 1963

The fight over equal pay legislation in the Kennedy years took place in a very different context from the earlier battles. The politics of the time welcomed new programmes, and equal pay fitted into the larger programme of the Kennedy administration both to revitalise the economy and to draw upon the resources women offered. By now, the question of whether working women would take jobs away from male breadwinners and set off a new depression had been answered: women worked in jobs different from those of men—jobs men didn't want.

Given the sexual segregation of the workplace, few women would benefit from equal pay legislation, but prevailing sentiment favoured giving those few the protection they deserved. In the last years of the Eisenhower administration, when social and economic obstacles had dissipated, equal pay bills fell victim not only to the objections of opponents but also to differences among supporters. In the Kennedy administration, the Women's Bureau gained the strength to lead the equal pay battle effectively. Its director, Esther Peterson, was both an assistant secretary of labour and a former lobbyist for the AFL-CIO. As such, she had authority within the administration and with women's organisations and labour unions, advantages her predecessors had lacked. Both context and structure now favoured the enactment of the first federal law to bar discrimination against women by private employers.

Since the Women's Bureau coalition had begun its campaign for equal pay legislation after World War II, the role of women in the paid labour force had changed and expanded dramatically. During the 1950s the demand for female workers had burgeoned, the result of growth in the clerical and service occupations, which employed women almost exclusively. Yet at the same time, the proportion of young single women seeking employment in the United States declined. The low birth rate of the 1930s meant that there were fewer young women in their twenties to take all the jobs designated as "women's work". Moreover, many young women now elected to go to college rather than work, and more of the others were getting married thus causing the pool of available single women in their twenties to evaporate further. Because the younger married women tended to stay home to care for their infants—a commonplace phenomenon with the explosion in the birthrate after World War II—employers had to forgo their preference for young, unencumbered female workers and offer jobs to older, married women with school-age children. Smaller families, the appearance of convenience foods, and the availability of various household appliances made it easier for wives and mothers to choose to work outside the home. The GI bill, which offered men incentives to stay in school, also encouraged employment of married women to supplement meagre family allowances. Between 1950 and 1960, the number of wives at work increased by 42 percent, from 21.6 percent in 1950 to 30.6 percent in 1960. As of March 1963, 41.5 percent of mothers with children between the ages of six and seventeen worked for wages, compared with 30.3 percent in 1950, a 37 percent increase. Mothers with children under the age of six raised their labour force participation rate from 14 percent in 1951 to 22.5 percent in 1963, a 61 percent jump. By 1961 approximately twenty-four million women were working, 34 percent of all workers. The Department of Labour predicted that by 1970 this number would swell to thirty million. One Labour Department economist in 1963 stated that the growing incidence of married women workers represented "the most significant employment trend in the country".

The employment of wives resulted, observers detected, in more egalitarian marriages and in greater political participation of women, but it did not expand women's employment choices, nor did it raise their wages. Women workers still tended to be clerks, service workers, factory operatives, domestic workers, nurses, and teachers. In 1960, the wages of full-time year-round women workers averaged only 60.6 percent those of men, down from 63.6 percent in 1957. Black women fared worst of all: their earnings were 42 percent of men's.

Organising Support

Against this backdrop, the Women's Bureau staff organised the quest for equal pay legislation in the new Congress. The outgoing Eisenhower administration, which for eight years had supported equal pay bills in vain, again submitted a proposal before Kennedy's inauguration. Immediately after, Peterson arranged for meetings with Democratic congresswomen, representatives of organised labour, and the members of the National Committee on Equal Pay to review the legislative situation. The retirement of Graham Barden, the unfriendly chairman of the House Education and Labour Committee, made the situation much more tractable: his replacement, Adam Clayton Powell, Jr., a black Democrat from New York, favoured the bill.

As before, the conflicts about the measure focused on two items: the coverage of employees and the mode of enforcement. Several Democratic congresswomen, including Edith Green (D-Oreg.), had introduced bills modelled on the broad coverage of the National Labour Relations Act (which applied to industries "affecting" interstate commerce). These bills granted enforcement authority to the secretary of labour. Two Republican legislators, Jessica Weis and Katharine St. George (both from New York), had introduced bills modelled on the narrower Fair Labour Standards Act (FLSA, which covered employers "engaged in" interstate commerce). Their proposals provided for judicial enforcement. The AFL-CIO had cleared the Green bill before its introduction, and equal pay advocates within the Department of Labour initially wanted the administration to support it as well, a course of action urged by experienced staffers to eliminate the problem of competing bills.

Under the direction of the Women's Bureau, opinion quickly coalesced around a compromise proposal. The administration bill would adopt the FLSA-based coverage of the Republican bills to facilitate administration by the Wage and Hour Division of the Department of Labour, which oversaw the FLSA; however, it would retain the provision of the Green bill that gave "cease and desist" powers to the secretary of labour, as the AFL-CIO wanted. The Solicitor's Office of the Labour Department agreed to draft the bill. In the meantime, the Women's Bureau set out to accumulate statistical evidence establishing the need for federal legislation—ostensibly a major impediment in the past. J.A. Beirne, president of the Communications Workers of America, wrote to Secretary of Labour Arthur Goldberg in February 1961 informing him that at past hearings the union had been "tremendously impressed by the lack of authoritative data on male-female wage differentials for workers doing the same work in a given plant or office location." Internal studies by the CWA showed no such wage differentials, according to Beirne; rather, discrimination took place in women's not being permitted to apply for the higher-paying jobs. Beirne expressed hesitation about supporting an equal pay bill without such data, attributing past failures to this omission. Beirne recommended that the government act to equalise employment opportunities in the event that widespread wage differentials could not be found.

So, while the AFL-CIO studied the administration's draft bill, the Women's Bureau wrote to dozens of women's organisations and labour unions, asking them to use their resources to supply specific examples of wage discrimination. Reluctant to employ instances only from unionised plants, Peterson requested the AFL-CIO's organisation director to have his staff look for cases from nonunion shops. In addition, promising confidentiality, the Women's Bureau wrote to state labour departments, hoping for instances from adjudicated cases or settlements. Finally, Peterson wrote to women who had complained to the bureau about wage discrimination in the past, asking them about their present situation and soliciting leads to cases.

With the Women's Bureau now actively engaged in shoring up the coalition and gathering data, Arthur Goldberg decided to turn over to the bureau the entire lobbying effort on the bill as well. The department's Legislative Liaison Office had no particular interest in it—it had been around "forever"—and he assumed the bureau would work harder at getting the bill through Congress. In March 1961 Esther Peterson hired Morag Simchak, a lobbyist for the United Rubber Workers, to take charge.

The White House Legislative Liaison Office also left the effort to the Women's Bureau. John Kennedy had supported equal pay legislation during his tenure in Congress, but without vigour. He introduced a bill in 1951 at the request of former House representative Mary T. Norton, who was then working as an aide to the secretary of labour, but did no more than that. In 1957, when he was chairman of the labour subcommittee of the Senate Committee on Labour and Public Welfare, he cosponsored an equal pay measure with Senator Wayne Morse and others but did not hold hearings on the bill despite a request to do so. A confidential listing of the standing of White House legislative proposals omitted equal pay legislation under both "major" and "minor" headings. Thus the "administration effort" on behalf of equal pay legislation became more and more localised in the Women's Bureau office at the Department of Labour.

The Women's Bureau managed at least to bring its regular

constituents into line. The AFL-CIO disliked the narrowed, FLSA-based coverage of the bill, but acquiesced. The National Committee on Equal Pay, composed of many of Peterson's old colleagues, including Caroline Davis of the United Automobile Workers, Mary Anderson, the first director of the Women's Bureau, Helen Berthelot of the Communications Workers, and Olya Margolin of the National Council of Jewish Women, quickly concurred. By mutual agreement, Edith Green, who had sponsored equal pay legislation ever since her election to the House of Representatives, was named chief sponsor in that body. Wayne Morse (D-Oreg.), an originator of equal pay legislation in 1945, and Patrick McNamara (D-Mich.), whose subcommittee would consider the bill, would introduce the bill in the Senate.

Although the department of Labour and the White House expressed solid support for the bill, other administration officials tried, albeit unsuccessfully, to block the measure. Under Secretary of Labour W. Willard Wirtz wrote Goldberg in early May 1961: "Arthur: I an *not* in favour of this proposal. I think it is utterly unrealistic and that if such a bill were adopted it would be the worst failure since the 18th Amendment. Nor am I persuaded that this is either necessary or good public relations". The Bureau of the Budget, too, expressed reservations about the need for such a bill and delayed its approval while awaiting cost estimates.

Nevertheless, by the end of July Esther Peterson was able to write to AFL-CIO legislative director George Riley that "things are moving along at last". The administration bill was sent to the House and Senate in August 1961. In his transmittal letter to the president of the Senate, Goldberg observed that unequal wages had an adverse impact on both purchasing power and worker morale, which in turn hindered production, a key concern of the Kennedy administration. Equal pay, Goldberg contended, would prevent employers from using women to undercut the wages of male workers and would bring the work-place closer to the ideals of American justice.

Equal pay legislation also received the endorsement of the President's Commission on the Status of Women, a move Peterson orchestrated. At its first meeting in February 1962, Eleanor Roosevelt, the commission chairman, commented: "I should think this was a fairly safe thing to take up," and she told the press that the commission believed that unequal wages for comparable work were "contrary to the concept of equality and justice in which we believe."

While the Women's Bureau staff shepherded the bill through legislative channels, data in support of the bill began to come in from the Women's bureau constituents. The American Association of University Women produced a study of men and women in executive positions that disclosed discriminating pay practices in many companies. Caroline Davis of the UAW supplied material about a recent strike that resulted in the reduction of pay differentials between men and women, not to zero, but to ten cents an hour. Hattie Trazenfeld of the BPW reported on cases collected from that organisation's membership, and the Women's Bureau discovered specific wage differentials in about a dozen union contracts from 1959 to 1961. Peterson herself sought cases as she travelled around the country. At one point, a manager told her that unequal pay scales were "equitable." When, over coffee, she pressed him for his meaning, he offered lame justifications, which she commended she did not understand. Finally he said to her: "Mrs. Peterson, don't do this to me. You know we pay them less because we can get them for less," an explanation Peterson often repeated in discussions with members of Congress.

Thus, proponents were well prepared for the nearings that took places in March 1962, before a select subcommittee on labour headed by Herbert Zelenko (D-N.Y.) of the House Education and Labour Committee. Arthur Goldberg led off, addressing himself to the principle of equal pay legislation, then Peterson offered individual stories and surveys of wages in particular cities, including a Women's Bureau study of work orders for public employment revealing 120 job requests that offered men higher wages than women. Representatives from both sides of the aisle spoke in favour, as did delegates of various labour unions who called for the bill's enactment in order to bring non-union shops and less enlightened unions than their own into line with the principle. Emma Guffey Miller, now chairman of the National Women's party, supported the bill as befitted a devoted Democrat but spent most of her testimony arguing for the Equal Rights amendment. (Privately, Miller called the measure "the so-called equal pay bill"; another NWP member characterised it as "a smart dodge for the people who want to spike the movement for real equality".) Katherine Peden, president of the National Federation of Business and Professional Women's Clubs, appeared for that organisation's 175,000 members and offered examples of unequal pay from BPW files. The American Association of University Women and the National Councils of Jewish, Catholic, and Negro Women also sent contingents. The National Association of Manufacturers did not attend but filed a statement affirming its belief in equal pay and its opposition to federal "intervention". Additional hearings also took place in New York, where such notables as Eleanor Roosevelt and Bette Davis testified, along with several more organisations. No one offered opposing arguments.

A clean bill incorporating changes suggested in the hearings received unanimous endorsement from the House committee. The administrative enforcement provision had been lost, which irritated the AFL-CIO, and a section excluding employers with fewer than twenty-five employees was added, but the committee included a new provision expressly forbidding employers to lower the wage rates of male employees to comply. During the House debate on the rule, Representative Katharine St. George (R-N.Y.) declared that she did not see how anyone could oppose the legislation: "It would be like being against motherhood". Nevertheless, many representatives had specific objections. Chief among them was the language of the key clause, requiring "equal pay for comparable work". In response, Katharine St. George proposed substituting the phrase "equal pay for equal work".

Bills concerning equal pay for women had always used the terminology "comparable work" requiring "comparable skills," rather than "equal work". Opponents of the bill objected that comparability would prove virtually impossible to determine, but advocates feared that "equal" would mean "identical", and that "slight and inconsequential" differences might be used to justify disparate wages. Few state equal pay laws applied only to indentical jobs, and General Order 16, promulgated by the War Labour Board in 1942, spoke of "comparable quality and quantity of work" in authorising equal wages for women workers. Supporters argued that formal job analysis and rating procedures, carried on in cooperation with labour and management, would establish "comparability" if necessary. This battle went to the conservatives, however: Republicans heavily supported St. George's amendment to change the wording and it passed 138 to 104.

During the House debate on the measure, several representatives offered additional amendments. Republican representative Charles Goodell (New York) moved to eliminate the provision prohibiting compliance through a lowering of wage rates, citing the "panic" of retailers, and the amendment passed 132 to 116. An amendment to add the words *or race* to the bill everywhere that *sex* appeared, offered by Charles S. Joelson (D-N.J.) was disallowed on a point of order, raised by Edith green, as not being "germane". At the close of the debate the House passed the bill by voice vote. No one had spoken on the floor against it.

House approval surprised and alarmed business groups. Unaware of the new impetus behind the bill, they had assumed it would meet the same it has before. The U.S. Chamber of Commerce, realising that it has been remiss in failing to take concerted action against the bill in the House, hastily organised a campaign to bottle up the bill in the Senate committee. "Nobody really was taking the bill very seriously, but suddenly it has become a reality", a chamber spokesman told the *Wall Street Journal.* The *Journal* attributed the bill's success to administration efforts and quoted a Senate Democrat as saying, "The Kennedy administration really wants this. They can build this up as a staggering social achievement.

As part of its eleventh-hour lobbying effort, the chamber devoted an issue of its bulletin to equal pay, assuring business leaders that their fear of equal pay legislation did not mean they were prejudiced. The chamber asserted that there were in fact many arguments against "coercive" federal power: for one, pay differentials often resulted from the "added costs" of employing women, caused by their supposedly higher rates of absenteeism and turnover and by state laws requiring special benefits such as rest periods. Federal legislation to compel equal pay would undoubtedly create more problems than it would solve, the chamber insisted. That the misbegotten bill had gotten as far as it did the chamber attributed to "Mrs. Peterson's twelve hour day".

In their attempt to stall action in the Senate, business groups confronted the chairman of the Senate subcommittee on Labour, Pat McNamara, and demanded hearings. McNamara refused. The chamber finally found an ally in the ranking minority member of the Senate Labour and Public Works Committee, Barry Goldwater (R-Ariz.), who succeeded in blocking committee approval. When McNamara finally agreed to amend the bill to permit employers to reflect "added costs" in wage differentials, Goldwater lent his support. Because it was too late to win committee endorsement, in early October McNamara offered the bill as a rider to a State Department construction bill already before the Senate and it passed.

Although the equal pay bill had for the first time won approval in both houses of Congress, McNamara's strategy ultimately failed. Because the Senate bill differed from the House bill, the legislation had to go to a conference committee. But the Senate action had created parliamentary problems: the bill to which McNamara appended the equal pay measure had been reported out of the Senate Foreign Relations Committee, whereas the House Education and Labour Committee had handled equal pay. With only nine days between the Senate vote and adjournment, committee jurisdiction could not be resolved and the bill died. The belated opposition of the business community, by stalling the bill in the Senate Committee for so long, resulted once more in the bill's demise. But this time the new backers the bill were not so easily undone.

Compromise and Victory

Peterson, Simchak, and the Women's Bureau staff started on a new bill immediately. Taking into account the various amendments of the administration bill offered in each house and the recommendations of the AFL-CIO, the new draft, again modelled on FLSA coverage, included the following provisions: enforcement by the secretary of labour, exemption of employers with fewer than twenty-five employees, prohibitions against compliance by wage cutting and against labour unions seeking unequal wage scales, use of the language "equal work" rather than "comparable work", a gradual elimination of wage differentials, and exclusion of offending firms from government contracts.

The draft bill represented a compromise. The AFL-CIO objected to FLSA coverage and to permitting employers to bring wages into line gradually. The Department of Labour disliked substituting "equal work" for "comparable work". Yet advocated of the legislation took the position that, for the moment, half a loaf was better than none.

With the replacement of Secreatary of Labour Arthur Goldberg by Under Secretary W. Willard Wirtz in September 1962, however, new problems appeared from within the administration. Goldberg had strongly backed the bill; Wirtz opposed it. With Wirtz running the shop, other equal pay opponents became bold. In response to a request for an opinion on the new bill, Walter Heller, chairman of the Council of Economic Advisers (CEA), notified the Bureau of the Budget that the council objected to the bill, citing a lack of "convincing evidence" and the possibility that "economic" reasons, such as the "added costs" of hiring women, might account for such differentials as did exist. Heller based his letter on an internal memorandum, written by Norman Simler of the CEA staff. Simler, who warned the council that fighting the bill was like "opposing virtue", accused the Labour Department of supporting the bill for its vote-getting appeal and failing to document its contention that women were indeed paid less than men, relying on "common knowledge" rather than hard data. Simler found the bill more objectionable now that it referred to "equal work" rather than "comparable work"; he doubted that many men and women actually did "equal" jobs and feared employers could therefore easily evade enforcement efforts. He predicted that the department would ultimately create another expensive bureaucracy that would not succeed in eliminating pay discrimination. "But even if it [the bill] could be administered and enforced", Simler argued, "no evidence is presented demonstrating a need for it."

Peterson responded aggressively to the CEA's contentions, asserting that Heller's reasoning revealed "a complete lack of understanding of not only the political but the economic aspects of the bill". After a telephone conversation with Peterson, Heller agreed "to take another look at it", and to have Simler call her as well. Her conversation with Simler disclosed that his research had been limited; he had neither looked at the report of the committee hearings nor asked the Women's Bureau for additional information. The day following Peterson's conversation with the two, the Council of Economic Advisers withdrew its letter to the Budget Bureau.

Both Simler and Heller remained unpersuaded, however. In a memorandum for the council, Simler summarised the evidence Peterson had offered to Congress in 1962. Although he included surveys of job-hiring orders with double pay scales, labour-management contracts that applied wage rates by sex, two private surveys of employers totalling more than two thousand firms of which one-third admitted to double pay standards, and a survey of salary schedules by the National Education Association showing one salary rate for men and another for women teachers in sixteen school districts, he insisted that the differing wage rates could reflect disparities in job content that the titles failed to disclose. He concluded: "What this all adds up to is that the Management Department does not have one shred of evidence, except possibly the 120 cases of job orders . . . , that there is discrimination in *wage rates* based on sex where men and women perform *equal* work on jobs requiring *equal* skill in the *same* place of employment". Still, Heller said, the Council of Economic Advisers would not enter "objection" to the bill.

Disturbed by the new opposition from within the administration, Peterson dealt with Wirtz directly. In a February 1963 meeting, he objected to the costs of enforcing the equal pay law. Perceiving a lack of sympathy on his part for women affected by such discrimination, Peterson argued that his objection to administrative enforcement would embarrass the administration vis-à-vis unions and women's organisations. Moreover, the amount of money requested for enforcement was small in comparison to other allocations. "It does not seem unreasonable", Peterson maintained, "to spend approximately the same amount of money the government now spends on paper clips and stapling machines in order to protect the pay of 24 million women members of the management force". Peterson argued also from the political standpoint—that women felt that pay and job discrimination affected them seriously and that such a bill would impress groups such as the BPW, possibly breaking them away from their traditionally Republican allegiance. She recognised that the bill constituted only a first step for women: "This Bill will *not* give most of them real relief, since it does not give them equal opportunity". But it would point the way to future steps.

Peterson prevailed; the Bureau of the Budget finally advised that it would not obstruct the bill. Despite the continuing objections of Secretary Wirtz and CEA chairman Heller, Peterson carried the administration bill to the Hill on February 14, 1963, where it was introduced in the House by Edith Green and in the Senate by Pat McNamara. The prohibition against compliance by lowering wages had been omitted because McNamara believed the bill included the injunction implicitly. The Labour Department continued to amass better evidence of the bill's need, and the AFL-CIO Executive Council issued a statement calling for prompt action without detrimental amendments. Frank Thompson, chairman of the House Select Subcommittee on Management (who kept material on the bill filed under *B* for "Broads"), scheduled hearings for the middle of March, hoping that, in view of the extensive hearings held the previous year, testimony would be brief.

This time, business representatives organised early. The Chamber of Commerce urged its members to write wire their representatives telling them that the bill would give the government "sweeping powers over industry" and make the secretary of labour "Prosecutor, Judge, and Jury". Manufacturers' associations met with Labour Department officials and complained that the new bill did not take into account the "added costs" of hiring women or the fate of small manufacturers who would go out of business if they to raise women's wages.

Representative Charles Goodell (R-N.Y.) sympathised with these complaints. Goodell himself believed the administration bill to be too vague; in conjunction with labour and industry representatives, particularly officials of Corning Glass Works, an important New York employer, Goodell offered a bill simply amending the Fair Labour Standards Act. As such, the bill contained no twenty-five employee test, it narrowed coverage by excluding all the exempted occupations included in section 13 of the FLSA, and it utilised the enforcement provisions of the FLSA, which meant that only courts could compel employers to comply.

During the hearings in March and April, Peterson and the bureau's allies testified against Goodell's approach. Amending the FLSA would bring undesirable consequences, they said, particularly the unavailability of administrative enforcement and the exclusion of several categories of employees from coverage. The AFL-CIO representative argue that even the coverage of the administration bill (which followed the FLSA in affecting only employers "engaged in" commerce) fell short; the labour organisation still preferred the broader scope of the National Labour Relations Act.

This time, four corporate executives spoke in opposition to any equal pay law, and five more submitted written statements. Their objections rested on the powers given the secretary of labour to "harass" businesses, the supposed added costs of hiring women, the anticipated difficulty of assessing equality of work, and the lack of a need for federal legislation. Some firms, though, reflecting an awareness of the likelihood that *some* bill would pass, testified in favour of legislation if it were to be an amendment to the Fair Labour Standards Act.

Business opposition to the administration measures was much more vocal than it had been in the fifties, when the bill had failed without it. After the hearings pressure mounted to assuage business fears by enacting equal pay legislation through revision of the Fair Labour Standards Act. Although the department of Labour feared this proposal might open up the FLSA to the less desirable amendments, advantages became apparent. By way of compromise, the administration bill had limited coverage to employers with twenty-five or more employees; because the FLSA applied to all employers with two or more employees "engaged in commerce", amending the FLSA would actually increase by about three million the number of employees covered. With business objection so strong, Peterson and others feared that administrative enforcement would be lost in the legislative process anyway, and the FLSA provided established investigative practices that often resulted in voluntary compliance before court action became necessary. Goodell's bill had the recorded support of many Republicans; it appealed to legislators because it was "simple"—it did not require new procedures or machinery. The Department of Labour began to consider any other prospect of passage unlikely.

After close consultation with Peterson, Simchak and other

Labour Department staff, the Senate and House committees decided to endorse amendment of the FLSA. On April 30, Pat McNamara introduced such a bill in the Senate, with Edith Green following in the House on May 6. Both bills prohibited discrimination on the basis of sex in the payment of wages for "equal work on jobs the performance of which requires equal skill, effort and responsibility, and are performed under similar working conditions", and neither permitted employers to lower wages rates to reach this goal. The act was to take effect one year from the date of passage. Both the House and the Senate committees reported the bills quickly and favourably, barely one week after their introduction, despite an attempt by the Chamber of Commerce to instigate further hearings because of "inadequate" consideration of this approach in the earlier hearings. In response to the congressional committee reports, Peterson stated: "There are advantages and disadvantages to this FLSA route, but the decision was made by the Congress and we believe the bills as reported out of committee are good ones". With little debate, the Senate passed the bill on May 17.

Peterson had consulted with the AFL-CIO before consenting to Goodell's proposal, and, reluctantly, the organisation supported the new bill. Welting to members of Congress, Andrew J. Biemiller, director of the department of Legislation, asked for their vote in favour but observed that the bill did not meet even "minimum requirements for equal pay legislation" and cautioned against any further weakening amendments. Yet Biemiller also stated that the organisation would support an amendment to delete a provision granting an extra one-year stay of the law in cases where the employees were covered by a union contract. The measures granted relief, claimed Biemiller, not to unions but to employers.

During the House debate at the end of May, few representatives spoke against the bill in general, although several offered specific amendments. Motions to forbid the secretary of labour to investigate without a written complaint and to permit employers to pass along "costs of hiring women" in wage differences both met defeat. Those amendments that were adopted did not eviscerate the bill: the House spelled out that wage differentials resulting from seniority, merit, or piece rate would not be illegitimate, and added a provision making labour unions culpable if they attempted to get an employers to agree to wage differentials based on sex. Many representatives commended the choice to amend the Fair Labour Standards Act over other methods of enactment. The bill in the House passed easily on May 23.

Senator McNamara, contradicting assertions made on the House floor, took pains to state for the record that the bill did not require "a pattern of violation" for an employers to be culpable and that the Senate did not construe "equal" to mean "identical". The Senate then concurred in the House amendments—the final legislative action—on May 28. Thus, eighteen years after its initial proposal an equal pay bill came before the president for his signature.

The long fight for an equal pay law culminated in a signing ceremony in the president's office on June 10, 1963, with several congresswomen, Wirtz, Peterson, Simchak, and Labour Department staff members, representatives of women's organisations, Mary Anderson, and Frances Perkins in attendance. In his remarks, drafted at the Labour Department, Kennedy observed that despite the work still to be done, the law represented a significant moment.

Although its focus was narrow, the Equal Pay Act marked the entrance of the federal government into the field of safeguarding the right of women to hold employment on the same basis as men. Traditionally, the business community had justified women's lower wages by claiming that women worked for "pinmoney", not for income to support their families. By making wage discrimination illegal, the federal government undermined this view and implicitly supported, for the first time, the contention that paid employment was consonant with a woman's obligations as wife and mother.

Women who had worked long and hard for equal pay legislation expressed deep gratitude to Peterson. Wrote Caroline Davis of the UAW:

> It could never have happened without the tremendous effort put forth on your part and the work of the women in your U.S. Women's Bureau under your expert guidance. Believe me I know, because for 15 years that I have been on the staff of the UAW we have worked to secure passage of a law, and at a time had high expectations, only to have [them] dashed before we got very far. This is indeed a great accomplishment on your part and you can rightfully be very proud that your influence played the greatest part in securing this victory.

Indeed, the leadership of the Women's Bureau proved crucial. The bureau forged a compromise by persuading women's organisations and labour groups to accept a bill lacking features they had considered vital and by quashing disunity in the administration. In its final form, the equal pay law guaranteed equal pay for "equal" rather than "comparable" work; it excluded employees not covered by the Fair Labour Standards Act; it contained no provision for administrative enforcement. Yet future amendments to the Fair Labour Standards Act extended coverage, and the procedures established by the Wage and Hour Division of the Department of Labour ultimately offered good results. Court decisions construed the meaning of "equal work" liberally, declining to apply the law solely to identical jobs: in the first ten years of its enforcement, 171,000 employees had been awarded $84 million in back pay alone under the provisions of the law.

The Women's Bureau coalition had succeeded in enacting its chief legislative objective through the advantages of a sympathetic social setting, an administration tied to its labour constituency, and effective leadership in Peterson and Goldberg. This particular combination of circumstances permitted the Women's Bureau coalition to achieve yet another of its goals: a commission on the status of women that had the power to reach beyond the narrow limits of an equal pay law and examine the whole question of women's status, even while draining away the minimal energy still fueling the Equal Rights Amendment.

5

The PCSW Versus the ERA

If the Equal Pay Act represented a "specific bill for a specific ill," the President's Commission on the Status of Women served as the Kennedy Administration's omnibus approach to matters affecting women's lives. Since 1946 the Women's Bureau coalition had sought such a commission, but before 1961 every attempt in congress to create a commission to examine the status of women had been derailed by the debate over the ERA. Esther Peterson, secretary of labour Arthur Goldberg, and their associates in the Department of Labour determined that such a fate would not befall the commission they proposed. Confident of the resources at their command, they contemplated instead a commission that, by taking a fresh approach to the problems confronting women, would do in the ERA.

One of the resources they possessed was the support of the president. All the previous efforts to establish a commission had looked to Congress to enact legislation, but that strategy had allowed ERA supporters to marshal their partisans to oppose the commission. When Peterson came to Goldberg with her idea for a commission, the secretary of labour offered a different idea: that the president establish the commission by executive order. With the Labour Department running this particular show, ERA supporters would not even know about the commission until it was a fait accompli.

The idea of an executive commission was not entirely new either. Several times since World War II, organisations had proposed presidential commissions to study ways to advance opportunities for women, though without success. In 1948 the American Association of University Women had asked President Truman to name a commission of outstanding men and women to recommend measures to integrate women into every phase of the preparedness programme. The National Security Resources Board rejected the proposal, saying: "It is recognised that there are no basic personnel techniques of unique applicability to women workers". The board insisted that the idea that women must be distinguished from other workers "represents one of the more potent obstacles to the general use of women workers". After the Korean conflict began, the AAUW reiterated its request, telling the president that a commission was needed to establish policy concerning the use of women in such emergencies, and that women should be integrated in the planning for the long-range defence effort. Again administration advisers concluded that "there is no special problem of 'women power'. Problems in utilising women are part and parcel of the total problem of utilising human resources."

The most important recommendation had come from the National Manpower Council (NMC) at Columbia University. In the 1957 study *Womanpower,* the council staff pointed out that, although the federal government had not taken a stand on the desirability of women's employment had not taken a stand on the desirability of women's employment, many statutes concerning, for example, taxation and licensing, had an impact on women workers. The NMC therefore recommended that the secretary of labour establish a committee to review "the consequences and adequacy of existing federal and state laws which have a direct bearing on the employment of women".

Eisenhower's Department of Labour, however, seemed loath to admit, by appointment of a commission, that it was not equal itself to the task the NMC proposed. Women's Bureau director Alice Leopold recommended that the secretary "utilise existing facilities, including both governmental agencies and interested non-governmental organisations" to look into the effect of legislation on women's employment. Leopold may have doubted her ability to control a commission composed of leaders of women's organisations and notable educators with whom she had few ties; yet if the director of the Women's Bureau recommended against appointing a commission on women, no other administration official was likely to overrule her. The secretary followed her advice, and the commission was not appointed.

Ideas for a commission under the Kennedy administration came from many sources. The New York Business and Professional Women's Club had written to the president on inauguration day to request the creation of a panel to discuss the utilisation of the skills of mature women. Kennedy turned the letter over to Esther Peterson, who replied that another, similar plan was being considered. With Peterson, Katherine Ellickson, formerly assistant director of the Social Security Department of the AFL-CIO, and Dollie Lowther Robinson, also longtime union employee now at the Women's Bureau, the coalition favouring a commission had strong voices. Robinson, a black woman, urged that the president express the same concern for women's opportunities as he had about racial discrimination; the commission would be such a vehicle. Secretary Goldberg took the plan to Kennedy.

Kennedy agreed to the idea, sympathetic to the general aims and recognising that his administration needed a programme for women. At the commission's first meeting, Kennedy explained his support: "Every two or three weeks", he said, "Mrs. May Craig [the Washington correspondent for the Portland, Maine, *Press Herald*] asks me what I am doing for women.

The president's commission had many other appealing

aspects. For one, it had the potential to do some good—the problems it pointed to were legitimate matters of concern. Kennedy was confident of the commission's leadership in the Labour Department, believing rightly that they would not allow the commission to embarrass him. The proposal also had virtually no costs to the administration. The commission's goals, so far as they were stated, were congruent with the goals of the administration, and the mere establishment of the commission committed the president only to examining the problems raised, not to a particular set of policy initiatives. Once proposals were made, he could pursue them with some insulation from criticism. They would, after all, represent the best judgement of a prestigious group of public leaders, including the most prominent exponent of the liberal Democratic position and the most highly respected woman in the country, Eleanor Roosevelt.

The former first lady's acceptance of the commission chair identified her—at long last—with Kennedy's administration, an endorsement the president had long sought. Everyone backing the plan agreed that only Eleanor Roosevelt could chair a presidential commission on the status of women. Her acquiescence gave it the seal of approval and smoothed out the long and troubled relationship she had with Kennedy. As early as 1950, Roosevelt had opposed the then representative over a bill he was sponsoring giving aid to Catholic schools. In 1956, when Kennedy made a bid for the vice-presidential nomination, she had made much of his failure to speak out against Joseph McCarthy, the senator from Wiconsin who was wreaking havoc with unsubstantiated charges of communist infiltration in the government. Later, Roosevelt and Kennedy became embroiled in a tense exchange over an allegation Roosevelt had made on television—that Joseph Kennedy was spending lavishly to buy the nomination for his son. Intensely hostile to Kennedy's father, who had infuriated her husband when he was president, and dedicated to the candidacy of Adlai Stevenson, she had been a powerful opponent during the primary campaign. She was slow to rally to Kennedy even after he won the nomination, and

Roosevelt's distance had been a constant irritant to the Kennedy team. But now she was officially on board. Apart from conducting meetings, Roosevelt did little of the actual work of the commission; she did, though, serve as an adviser, make herself available for publicity purposes, and sign letters. When she died in November 1962, the administration decided not to appoint another chair, stating simply that there could be "no adequate replacement".

Under the leadership of the Women's Bureau, the plan to appoint a commission to investigate the status of women, after so many years of proposals for legislative and executive action, came finally to fruition. The Women's bureau staff drew up a comprehensive programme, and Peterson, Goldberg, and the White House staff selected the eleven men and fifteen women participants, making sure to acquire people who would ultimately develop a programme the White House could endorse.

Commission membership represented the mainstream opinion of the Women's Bureau coalition and included several key administration officials. Eleven members came from the government, including Peterson, who held the position of executive vice-chairman, the attorney general, the chairman of the Civil Service Commission, the secretaries of the Departments of Commerce, Agriculture, Labour, and Health, Education, and Welfare, and four members of Congress, two Republican and two Democrat. Officers of the National Councils of Jewish, Catholic, and Negro Women and the National Council of the Churches of Christ spoke for middle-class women reformers. Two more members came from labour unions. Two college presidents, Mary Bunting of Radcliffe College and Henry David of the New School for Social Research, represented the world of higher education. (Under Bunting's direction, Radcliffe had instituted a new programme to permit older women to return to college, and David had been executive director of the National Manpower Council when it published *Womanpower*.)

The commission also included Caroline Ware, a historian

who had been fired in 1935 from a summer teaching job at the University of Wyoming because she was married (to Gardiner Means, a New Deal economist). The incident had engendered a great deal of publicity because Ware fought the dismissal, gaining the support of the National Association of Women Lawyers, the BPW, the American Federation of Teachers, the National Woman's party, and several other organisations but to no avail. Margaret Hickey, the public affairs editor of the *Ladies' Home Journal,* also served. As a past president of the pro-ERA National Federation of Business and Professional Women's Clubs, Hickey appeared to favour the ERA, but only Marguerite Rawalt, an attorney and a member of many pro-ERA groups, endorsed the amendment openly. A representative of the progressive business firm Kaiser Industries and one political appointee placed on the commission at the request of Vice-President Lyndon Johnson made up the balance of the membership. Dr. Richard A. Lester, a Princeton University economist who had worked on the Kennedy campaign, was appointed vice-chairman.

President Kennedy established the President's Commission on the Status of Women on December 14, 1961. In his executive order, written at the Women's Bureau, the president contended that "prejudices and outmoded customs" prevented the "full realisation of women's basic rights" and hindered their ability to make their fuliest contribution to the national welfare. He pointed out that women traditionally had "served with distinction" in times of national emergency, only to be treated as marginal in times of peace. The creation of the commission recognised, he said, that women were entitled to "develop their capabilities and fulfil their aspirations on a continuing basis irrespective of national exigencies". The twenty-six-member commission was charged with reviewing progress and making recommendations in six arenas: employment policies and practices of the federal government; employment policies and practices of federal contractors; social insurance and tax laws; labour legislation; political, civil, and property rights; and new and expanded services necessary for women as wives, mothers, and workers. The commission's report was due October 1, 1963.

In his accompanying remarks, the president expressed his hope that the commission would indicate what needed to be done to demolish the barriers to women's full participation in the nation. Progress, he said, would require the "cooperation of the whole community", through legislation and the provision of needed services. He promised to make the federal government "a show case of the feasibility and value of combining genuine equality of opportunity on the basis of merit with efficient service to the public". The federal career service would henceforth be maintained, he declared, "in every respect without discrimination and with equal opportunity for employment and advancement".

Because the commission met only eight times in the two years of its existence, the Women's Bureau and commission staff exerted a great deal of influence. They implemented and commission requests, planned meetings, answered mail, communicated with other government agencies between meetings, developed position papers, and reviewed recommendations. Commission staff and officials also conferred with the White House over questionable proposals.

Confident that the commission would yield good results, the White House supported it enthusiastically. At the commission's first meeting, held at the Executive Mansion, the president assured the members of his backing: "I can't imagine any more important assignment—not merely for women, but for members of Congress, organised labour, women's organisations themselves, religious groups, and all the rest", he said. "I promise you that we are strongly behind you in all your work". In May 1962 he reiterated his interest in the commission's work on Eleanor Roosevelt's television programme, "Prospects of Mankind". Kennedy, moreover, never refused a request made of him by the commission, a happenstance undoubtedly aided by the fact that Esther Peterson cleared all such appeals with the White House before they were proffered.

In order to broaden its support among women's

organisations, the commission agreed at its first meeting to set up sub-committees composed of experts in various areas. The staff named seven committees after the subjects listed for investigation in the executive order: federal employment; private employment; civil and political rights; protective labour legislation; social insurance and taxes; home and community; and education. Each committee was chaired by a commission member, and most had at least one other member on its rolls. Like the commission, the eighty-nine committee members included educators, lawyers, and members of womens' organisations, labour unions, business firms, and state governments. The committee system gave many individuals and organisations a feeling of involvement in the commission's outcome.

Still, Esther Peterson, who guided the development of the commission within the Kennedy administration, realised that the dispute over the Equal Rights Amendment could easily wreck this commission, as it had all the other commission proposals. She knew that if the commission opposed the amendment at its outset, pro-ERA organisations would be unwilling to cooperate, and no consensus would emerge on an effective plan to help women. Although Peterson herself opposed the Equal Rights Amendment, she wanted to keep the conflict from destroying a serious effort at addressing the many conflicts, burdens, and obstacles confronting American women. Therefore, in contrast to the 1947 bill to establish a commission, the President's Commission on the Status of Women did not begin with an overt declaration against the constitutional amendment; Peterson promised, rather, that it would examine the issue "objectively".

The Equal Rights Amendment and the 1960 Campaign

John Kennedy agreed with the Women's Bureau coalition on the ERA. In 1957 the then senator had told the Massachusetts Committee for the Equal Rights Amendment that he could not declare in favour of the amendment although he believed in "non-discriminatory treatment of women". He wrote: "There is still, I humbly acknowledge, some question in my mind as to the most appropriate method of insuring real equality for women". In 1958 he explained to a constituent who requested his support for the resolution, "My experience in the field of protective labour legislation has made me somewhat wary about over-all solutions to problems which do not always lend themselves to easy or simple formulas". He assured her, however, that he continued "emphatically" to favour equal opportunity for women. During the preconvention presidential race, the senator declined to comment directly on the ERA.

Although attached to the Kennedy campaign, Esther Peterson was less circumspect. She was still working as a legislative representative for the Industrial Union Divison of the AFL-CIO, and from this position she headed the alliance to prevent the Democratic convention from endorsing the amendment in the 1960 party platform. Peterson testified before the platform committee on behalf of twenty-four national organisations, contending that real equality required measures that distinguished between men and women. "Specific bills for specific ills," she declared, was the better way to go. Peterson listed three principal objections to the ERA: it would nullify protective labour legislation at a time when increasing numbers of women in the labour force made the need for such laws more acute; it would create confusion in legislation concerned with marriage, property, and personal status; and it would fail to address the major forms of discrimination that were the result of custom. She asked the platform committee instead to endorse equal pay legislation and the pursuit of equal opportunity without disturbing protective labour laws.

The organised opposition surprised the National Woman's party, which had not been confronted by its opponents at the platform hearings since 1948. The NWP told the platform committee that renunciation of the ERA, in view of the Democratic Party's past commitment to it, would be "unprecedented and incredible". With support from the National

Federation of Business and Professional Women's Clubs and the General Federation of Women's Clubs, Emma Guffey Miller, chairman of the NWP, pointed out that past efforts showed that it would take more than a hundred years to repeal, law by law, the fourteen hundred statutes that discriminated against women. Moreover, she asserted, without the constitutional amendment subsequent state legislatures could reenact each one.

To Miller's dismay, the Democratic drafting committee accepted enough of the opposing argument to endorse, not the Equal Rights Amendment, but "equal treatment" for women. Incenced, Miller labelled the language "impossible" and meaningless. Working with representative William Green of Philadelphia, she managed to get the plank amended in the full platform committee, of which she was also a member. The plank read in its final form: "We support legislation which will guarantee to women equality of rights under the law, including equal pay for equal work". Despite the alteration, the platform represented success for opponents of the ERA. A statement in support of a constitutional amendment, which had appeared in every platform since 1944, had been eliminated.

The National Woman's party simply reused to acknowledge the defeat. As a member of its national council explained, "The wording, . . . though not so specific as 'Amendment,' does we feel include an amendment as a means of bringing about 'equality under the law' ". The language of the plank, she insisted, did not represent a victory for ERA enemies. Ignoring the facts, the NWP maintained that the Democrats had endorsed the ERA in 1960.

After the platform battle, the NWP sought Kennedy's personal endorsement of the ERA. Emma Guffey Miller, ultraloyal Democrat and chief advocate of the ERA within the Democratic Party wrote to John Kennedy that she was extremely concerned because Vice-President Richard M. Nixon, the Republican nominee, had delivered a prompt statement asking for "widespread support" of the Amendment. Miller advised

Kennedy to announce quickly in favour of the ERA and to point out publicly that the Democratic platform surpassed the Republicans' on women's rights. Labour opposition to the ERA, she counselled him, came not from chivalrous concern for the well-being of mothers but from male fears of lost jobs.

Wringing an affirmation of the ERA from John Kennedy proved difficult, however. Not only had Kennedy himself declined to support the ERA theretofore, but campaign letters on women's rights had to meet Esther Peterson's approval. Kennedy's reply to Miller, which Peterson checked over, thanked her for the opportunity to make a statement "regarding equal rights for women". Expressing his belief in equal rights for all "regardless of race, creed, colour, or sex," he quoted the platform plank and stated his full approval of it. The letter concluded: "You have my assurance that I will interpret the Democratic platform . . . to bring about, through concrete actions, the full equality for women which advocates of the equal rights amendment have always sought". The letter did not contain any statement of support for the Equal Rights Amendment.

Annoyed, Miller took the matter into her own hands. Although she had few ties to the Kennedy campaign (she had supported Lyndon Johnson in the primary battle), as a Democratic Committee member from Pennsylyania she had many friends at DNC headquarters. Miller amended the letter in pen and had a colleague deliver it to the DNC. There, an assistant to the chairman of the publicity committee had it typed on the Kennedy campaign letterhead and signed, presumably by machine, without the knowledge of the Kennedy campaign staff or of Peterson. The new letter read: "Thank you for providing me with an opportunity to make a statement regarding the equal rights amendment. . . . You have my assurance that I will interpret the Democratic platform . . . to bring about, through concrete actions including the adoption of the Equal Rights Amendment, the full equality for women which advocates of the equal rights Amendment have always sought."

In this manner, John Kennedy's "support" for the Equal Rights Amendment became a matter of official record. Peterson was outraged, but the Kennedy campaign let the matter drop, unwilling to expose internal conflict or inefficiency.

Miller won the battle, but the announcement that Esther Peterson was to head the Women's Bureau suggested that she would lose the war. When press reports intimated that Kennedy intended to appoint Peterson as Women's Bureau director, the National Woman's party was aghast. Emma Guffey Miller tried to organise a movement against Peterson and wrote to the president that this appointment was inconsistent with his stated support of the ERA, a disingenuous argument at best. Miller, who had no influence at the White House, did not succeed in harming Peterson.

The PCSW: An Alternative to the ERA

Peterson, in the meantime, found herself in a good position to make Miller miserable. In April, with eighty-two House resolutions on the ERA in the hopper, she told a *Washington Post* reporter that rather than having the ERA she would like to see a committee of the "best brains in the country" assay the status of women and recommend ways to improve it. She expressed her confidence that if all the women's organisations, pro and con, would discuss the conflict over women's legal place, a solution would appear. "If we sit down and talk this over", she said, "I feel sure we can work out a way to achieve our goals".

While the commission was being planned, Peterson cautioned presidential aide Myer Feldman to have his letter writers stick to the platform and omit any mention of the "nuisance" amendment in responding to letters from ERA supporters. She realised, she said, that the issue amounted to "peanuts", but the "pile of peanuts" was growing pretty big and the proponents were intensifying their efforts. Indeed, Miller, who scoffed at Peterson's offer of compromise, told her co-workers at the NWP to barrage secretary of Labour Arthur Goldberg with letters in order to "counteract" Peterson's influence, a campaign doomed to fail. Miller regarded Goldberg as "very broadminded"—but Peterson authorised the secretary's answers to letters from ERA supporters, and she used the exact language of the original Kennedy campaign letter, endorsing the Democratic platform and full equality for women but not the Equal Rights Amendment.

In the meantime, the ERA languished in Congress. Although 135 members of the House had introduced ERA resolutions by the fall of 1961, they did so with the knowledge that House Judiciary chair Emanuel Celler would not permit the bill to be reported. The seventeen Senate sponsors knew likewise that the upper chamber would agree to the amendment only with Carl Hayden's rider preserving "benefits" for women. Still, Miller viewed Peterson as the ERA's greatest threat. We must find some way to shut her up, at least from opposing what our platform and President have endorsed," she told a friend.

Peterson did not shut up; instead, she and her colleagues used the presidential commission on women to stop the ERA dead in its legislative tracks. Peterson reasoned that congress would not be likely to act on the amendment while the matter was under consideration by a presidential panel. In addition, she presumed that eventually the commission would offer substitute recommendations that would stymie the amendment's progress.

But obstructing the ERA was not the commission's chief objective; the Hayden rider had already taken care of that. The creators of the commission intended it primarily to devise an alternative programme to improve women's status. Unfortunately, as they saw it, the ERA dispute had always made such a goal impossible.

From the very first discussions about the commission early in 1961, its creators worried about protecting the commission from being "diverted" from its task by the argument over constitutional equality. Throughout the spring, the Women's Bureau staff, Peterson, and Katherine Ellickson of the Social Security Department of the AFL-CIO refined arguments in favour of a commission, hoping to devise a plan that women's organisations would deem acceptable, regardless of their position on the ERA. One staffer observed that "there is a good bit of evidence to suggest that the objectives of most women's groups with respect to women's status are the same, despite differences expressed by those who favour or oppose the Equal Rights Amendment."

When Peterson presented the plan to the White House, she began by arguing that "the appointment by the President of a Commission on women in our American democracy would substitute constructive recommendations for the present troublesome and futile agitation about the 'equal rights' Amendment." But more than that, she asserted, the commission would "help the nation to set forth before the world the story of women's progress in a free, democratic society, and to move further towards full partnership, creative use of skills and genuine equality of opportunity." Peterson told White House aide Myer Feldman that trade union women, professional women, and congressional staff had all greeted the idea with enthusiasm. But the commission could succeed only if the ERA dispute did not undermine it.

Therefore, Peterson decided, the PSCW would, in contrast to past commission proposals, begin without taking an overt stand on the issue. In her remarks at the announcement ceremony, Peterson paid tribute to Emanuel Celler, who had first introduced a bill proposing a national commission on women in 1947—but the Celler bill had included a policy statement endorsing statutes that distinguished women from men if the laws were "reasonably based on differences in physical structure, biological, or social function." This statement established before the fact that such a national commission would necessarily oppose the ERA, which was designed to strike down laws based on just such characteristics. The executive order creating the President's Commission on the Status of Women contained no such phrase indicating a preconceived position.

Peterson's plan paid off. The president's commission won

enthusiastic support from the influential BPW, as well as from many pro-ERA organisations. Congress members and women's organisations joined the BPW in expressing widespread interest in the commission, and women in the federal government felt encouraged by the new policy the president had enunciated. Caroline Davis, director of the Women's Division of the United Automobile Workers, wrote to Peterson: "Congratulations[;] you did it. This is a victory that we have long waited for". In an editorial, the *Washington Post* praised Kennedy for creating the "blue ribbon panel," declaring that the country could not afford to waste the trained talent of women. The *Christian Science Monitor,* observing that Kennedy had been criticised for failing to appoint women, crediting him with launching a "distaff 'fair deal'".

Not everyone shared the enthusiasm, however, Despite Peterson's expression of esteem and a letter from Arthur Goldberg telling him that the presidential commission represented the "fruition" of his efforts, Emanuel Celler took the commission to task. He noted its appearance with interest, he said, but he wanted to "sound a warning" that he would oppose "any effort on the part of this group to revive any campaign for the adoption of the so-called Equal Rights Amendment which is an 'Unequal Rights Amendment.' " Celler, perhaps because of the absence of the biological function clause, apparently did not recognise the commission's origins in his own proposal. He went on to vilify the amendment, declaring that "mores have set off women from men and no constitutional Amendment could alter them". He expressed his hope that the commission would not be "pressurised" to raise the "specter" of the ERA.

The National Woman's party also viewed the commission with suspicion, but for reasons more realistic than Celler's. Emma Guffey Miller correctly judged that the commission arose partly from Peterson's distress over Kennedy's "endorsement" of the ERA during the campaign, and Miller saw to her own dismay that Peterson was now "riding high, wide and handsome" within the administration. Alice Paul presciently explained to a questioner that the commission had been set up to prevent the adoption of the amendment and that ERA opponents would urge Congress members to delay action on the amendment until the commission had issued its report.

Opponents of the amendment did just that. The White House reported that the president would not comment on the amendment until the commission had concluded its work, and Arthur Goldberg asked Emanuel Celler to defer House Judiciary Committee activity on the ERA until the commission report was submitted. Celler in turn recommended to the Senate Judiciary Committee that it wait for the report, and Carl Hayden made the same request to the full Senate. Although the Senate Judiciary Committee reported the ERA favourably in August 1962, the Eighty-seventh Congress took no further action on it. An NWP member reported to Miller that both adversaries and advocates of the ERA in Congress with whom she had spoken "say frankly that they are not going to 'jump the gun' " on the president's commission.

Of course, there was never a chance that the commission would endorse the Equal rights amendment, despite its claim to be approaching the study of the ERA without prejudice. By design, too many commissioners came from labour or women's groups that opposed it. Because a body with no ERA supporters would lack credibility, Marguerite Rawalt, a past president of the BPW and a member of the National Woman's party, had been appointed, but she was the only certain ERA supporter of the membership of twenty-six. In addition, Peterson, Ellickson, and the Women's Bureau staff maintained a careful watch over the commission, monitoring proposals and making the administration position clear.

Although she knew Peterson would not allow many ERA supporters on the commission, Emma Guffey Miller, Democratic National Committee member and NWP chairman, did not take her exclusion philosophically. She brought her displeasure to the attention of John Bailey, chairman of the

DNC, and to Governor David L. Lawrence of Pennsylvania, a state in which the Guffeys and Millers had significant political clout. Lawrence confidently wrote to the White House asking that Miller be given a seat on the commission, but to his surprise he received a letter, drafted by Peterson, regretfully denying his request but offering Miller a seat on the commission's subordinate body, the Committee on Civil and Political Rights. Even this appointment did not come to pass, because Edith Green, the committee chairman, vetoed Miller's participation. Miller Continued her efforts to win a place on the commission until its conclusion, but Peterson squelched her petitions without much difficulty, explaining to the White House staff that the commission contained no political members except members of Congress and the cabinet. Furthermore, Peterson said, Marguerite Rawalt represented Miller's point of view. Miller's extended campaign to become a member of the Commission came to nothing.

Understandably, tension between Peterson and the National Woman's party remained high. Miller bitterly resented Peterson's station within the administration. An informant had told her, to her disgust that "no woman has an entree at the White House unless Esther Peterson . . . introduces her"; although this was an overstatement, the White House did customarily check such matters with her. Indeed, Peterson's instructions caused a White House aide to deny an appointment to an NWP member the president himself had promised to meet. For her part, Peterson viewed the National Woman's party with increasing disdain. She told Assistant Secretary of Labour Daniel Fadrick Moynihan and Lee White, a White House aide, that the NWP was a "paper organisation, with no standing with substantial women's organisations". The ERA was introduced each session, she said—"tongue-in-cheek"—because male legisilators hesitated to declare themselves against women, and the NWP consistently met with defeat despite the fact that "the little ladies marched the corridors from the first day of the session to its end." Nevertheless, because the Commission was ostensibly neutral, the warfare was covert. Peterson promised NWP correspondents that the subject of the ERA would be approached with an open mind. "As a member," she wrote, "I want to take this opportunity to assure you that the Commission has undertaken a completely objective study of this question".

Sequestering the ERA

If the commission did not in fact approach the subject of the ERA with an open mind, neither did it consider the subject lightly or arrive easily at the stand it took. The Women's Bureau and the commission staff recognised that, improperly handled, the dispute over the ERA could still make the commission fruitless. Even the commission members, many of whom were not privy to Peterson's rationale for the Commission's establishment, realised the dangers. Hyman Bookbinder, representing the secretary of commerce, broached the issue at the first meeting, feeling, he said, like "the proverbial fool who likes to move in where angels fear to tread". Remarking that the amendment had "divided the country" for years, he asserted that "if this Commission does nothing else [but] get an accommodation of views on this difficult and delicate area, we will have made a substantial contribution". Viola Hymes, president of the National Council of Jewish Women, agreed that the ERA had been "the most divisive . . . issue . . . among women's organisations", which had not re-examined their positions on it for twenty-five years. The commission would, she felt, "enable the women's organisations to take a new look in the light of developments and changes which will be very helpful". "Maybe", she suggested, "the women's groups will get together". To this Peterson declared: "It will be worth the Commission if we do it".

But for the commission to unite women's groups on this issue, it first had to make sure it would not itself be torn apart by it. Indeed, the planners evolved a way to prevent such an outcome—by sequestering the highly loaded discussion so that it did not supplant the rest of the commission's work. The commission turned the issue over to one of seven subunits it had established, the Committee on Civil and Political Rights. Because no public statement on the ERA would be made until the commission concluded its work, the other six committees could address the many additional problems women faced without themselves becoming embroiled in the conflict over constitutional equality.

As a result of this strategy, the Committee on Civil and Political Rights became the first commission body to confront the problem of the ERA directly. It did so in an exceedingly civilised fashion. Representative Edith Green, an ERA opponent, chaired the committee, although Marguerite Rawalt, the commission's one ERA advocate, took over when Green turned her attention to her re-election campaign. Peterson had appointed Rawalt to the commission because she considered her a sensible and thoughtful advocate of the ERA; Rawalt, in her turn, respected Peterson's directness and her commitment to improving women's employment laws. Committee membership, apart from the two commission members, included two representatives of labour unions, six members of the legal profession, most of them opposed to the ERA, and three presidents of pro-ERA women's organisations. ERA supporters were outnumbered, but at least they were represented.

The committee met for the first time in May 1962 and quickly established pointedly even-handed procedures for dealing with the ERA. Like the other commission subunits, the Committee on Civil and Political Rights began to accumulate data, in the form of returned questionnaires from women's organisations (on both sides of the ERA controversy), staff papers, and the findings of committee members' own research. The committee decided to invite four organisations—two groups favouring the amendment (the National Woman's party and the BPW) and two opposed (the American Association of University Women and the American Nurses Association)—to present their opinions on the ERA at the next meeting.

A Compromise Proposal

Unexpectedly, however, a member of the Civil and Political Rights Committee offered yet another approach to the matter of constitutional equality. Pauli Murray, a black attorney long associated with the civil rights movement, volunteered to write a memorandum detailing a strategy to get a court ruling that discriminatory state laws violated the Fourteenth Amendment. One of the few explicit connections between the civil rights movement and the federal quest for equity for women in the early 1960s. Murray's proposal offered, she said, an alternative to choosing one side or the other of the controversy. Murray thought the commission could thus avoid both conflict with the "very influential" National Woman's party and the waste of effort in attempting to win ratification of the ERA from three fourths of the state legislatures, which she viewed as impossible. Murray suggested instead that the commission recommend a concerted effort to pursue litigation of a case involving a discriminatory state law, with the goal of having the Supreme Court decide that arbitrary discrimination against women violated the Fourteenth Amendment in the same way racial bias did. The problem, as Murray saw it, was not that some laws distinguished between men and women, but that those that did failed to take into account differences among groups of women, such as those with children and those without. A ruling under the Fourteenth Amendment would provide the flexibility to maintain appropriate laws relating to women, while abolishing those that simply hampered women's right to function in the public sphere. In reviewing previous court cases, Murray argued that past decisions had not revealed a consistent pattern and that the Court might be willing to make a ruling distinguishing among groups of women if persuaded by a "Brandeis-type brief" discussing the changing roles of women. She proposed that either the American Civil Liberties Union or the Justice Department compile such a brief with the assistance of a commission-sponsored Legal Advisory Committee.

At the request of Esther Peterson, Pauli Murray presented her plan to the full commission at its October meeting. Impressed with her suggestions, the members decided to distribute an expanded version of her memorandum to attorneys in the Justice Department. Concern arose over the plan's implications for protective labour legislation, but Murray herself asserted that these laws should remain undisturbed.

In the expanded version of her paper, Murray explained that a new differentiation needed to be drawn between laws "genuinely protective of the family and maternal functions" and those that discriminated "unjustly" against women as individuals. The courts, she counselled, had not theretofore made distinctions among women, assuming that all would consider their maternal and family functions primary. True freedom of choice would permit women to develop different abilities if they so chose. Murray argued that the principle developed in the 1908 case *Muller* v. *Oregon*, which permitted states to enact laws aimed exclusively at women, had inappropriately been extended to institutionalise a virtual "separate but equal doctrine" for women. Laws could appropriately classify citizens by sex, she maintained, when the law protected "maternal and family functions" and applied only to women who performed those functions, when it protected the health of women or compensated for women's traditionally disadvantaged position, or when the differential treatment did not "imply inferiority". Murray suggested that a statute to protect future mothers could legitimately single out "women of child-bearing age"; she therefore did not envision the total equality sought by advocates of the Equal Rights Amendment. Nevertheless, she still affirmed the need to proscribe arbitrary classification by sex in state codes. Peterson regarded Murray's proposal with great hope. "You must know how grateful I am to you for this work", she wrote her. "I feel in my bones that you are making history".

Aware of the controversial nature of the proposal, and therefore of the necessity of frequent consultation with interested women's organisations, the Committee on Civil and Political

Rights invited fifteen women's organisations, including the National Woman's party, to appear before it in March to address the Fourteenth Amendment strategy, the ERA, and the state-by-state approach to women's legal status. Murray was hopeful of reaching an accord. She observed that in the past the advocates of both the national commission and the ERA had *assumed* that the Fourteenth Amendment could not reach discrimination based on sex. "The controversy over the Equal Rights Amendment seemed to force people who espoused the same goals into rigid positions and dissipated energies which might have gone toward a development of standards for the concept of equal status," she said. "[This controversy] can be avoided if we can get a consensus of sound alternatives."

But agreement was hard to come by. The American Association of University Women asserted that it still preferred the state-by-state approach. The American Nurses Association reasserted its stand against the ERA but said it did not feel qualified to comment on the Murray proposal. The National Council of Jewish Women both reiterated is objection to the ERA and took exception to the Murray recommendation. The NCJW spokeswoman, Mrs. Samuel Brown, predicted that the procedure would be "time-consuming, costly and laborious without any assurance that the results will be entirely satisfactory." Brown found the plan fundamentally lacking in two ways: it equated racial discrimination, which was always bad, with differential treatment based on sex, which was sometimes desirable; and it assumed that women's organisations, which had never before been able to agree on what constituted "discrimination", would now unite on a definition.

ERA proponents were no more enthusiastic. Although the National Woman's party agreed to appear at the committee hearing, the members evinced a deep distrust of the proceeding. Margery Leonard declined Emma Guffey Miller's request to represent the NWP, saying, "I wouldn't mind the time, effort and money involved in such an undertaking if I could feel it would do any real good. [But the Commission] is controlled by our arch enemy. The Commission was handpicked." Leonard asserted that even Marguerite Rawalt—an NWP member—was not their advocate: "The fact that she is on the Commission shows she is no friend of ours". Other NWP members contended that Pauli Murray, a black woman, was primarily concerned with the movement for racial equality and that she apparently intended "to hitch that wagon to our Equal Rights Amendment star," which would "spell disaster for our hopes". One party officer believed, in a staggering misperception of reality, that black civil rights groups wanted to use the ERA struggle "as a springboard for their own propaganda". Finally, however, the NWP did send two representatives to the committee meeting, at which the NWP, the BPW, the American Medical Women's Association, and the National Association of Women Lawyers backed the ERA, arguing that the Supreme Court had not in the past been amenable to making the sort of ruling that Murray advocated.

Of the groups asked, only the National Council of Catholic Women endorsed the Murray approach, but at the same time it emphasised the necessity of recognising differences between men and women. It approved of wider access for women to the world of politics and paid labour, especially in the fields of education and social work, but it cautioned, "It must be remembered that the most important function of woman will always be associated with home and family." Although man and woman were equal in dignity before God, the council asserted, their natures differed and women did not have the same ability to "wage that struggle for survival which still prevails in all walks of life". Women's organisations thus seemed to feel no impulse to abandon their prior positions to unite behind Murray's plan.

Nevertheless, as the discussion continued, the committee appeared convinced that, with the Fourteenth Amendment approach, women could have the protection of both the Constitution and state labour statutes. Its members felt sure that the Court would uphold statutes such as support laws requiring husbands to provide for their families—which would not be permissible under the ERA—and still strike down "unreasonable" legal distinctions. Respectful of differing viewpoints, and without an established position to defend or a history of personal antagonism, the committee could reach for a compromise.

The ERA—"Need not Now be Sought"

But even as the committee sought a new route toward constitutionally based equality, it still felt obliged to make a statement about the Equal Rights Amendment. At the March 1963 meeting committee member Frank Sanders, a Harvard University Law School professor, insisted that, with the amendment now under consideration by Congress, they had a duty to take a stand on the controversial item. "This has been an eternal political question", he told them. "There has been no Congress when this hasn't been pending before it. . . . Here is an expert body that spent two years and a hell of a lot of the government's money". Congress, he claimed, would want to know the committee's views. Esther Peterson said with Sanders that Congress expected guidance from the commission, and other committee members agreed that the situation demanded a declaration. Pauli Murray, however, demurred, still suggesting some way of dealing with the issue short of polarisation, which had stymied any action in the past. She explained, moreover, that if the Court refused to rule as she hoped under the fourteenth Amendment, she herself would advocate the ERA.

Although Peterson said she was reluctant to influence the committee's position, she nevertheless made the Department of Labour's views known. Pauli Murray asked whether the Labour Department would object to mention of the ERA as one of many alternatives. Peterson initially replied: "I think you should express yourselves on this. I have tried to stay out"; but she continued, "The Department of Labour does feel that protective labour legislation is seriously threatened if an equal rights amendment were passed." Peterson endorsed the suggestion that the committee approve the principle expressed in the ERA while indicating "dissatisfaction" with "any formulation presently in effect" coupled with an affirmative approach under the Fourteenth Amendment. At the end of the March meeting, the committee asked a subcommittee composed of Pauli Murray, Marguerite Rawalt, and three others to draft a recommendation on the subject of constitutional equality, which it could propose to the full commission.

The subcommittee resolution affirmed the need for constitutional recognition of women's equality before the law and ducked the issue of the Equal Rights Amendment. The recommendation read: "Equality of rights under the law for all persons, male or female, is so basic to democracy and its commitment to the ultimate value of the individual that it must be reflected in the fundamental law of the land". Pauli Murray proposed an additional statement that declared: "the Commission also believes that legal distinctions between the sexes not reasonably justified by differences in physical structure or by maternal function are violative of this constitutional principle", but the subcommittee rejected it. The subcommittee expressed its sentiment that the principle of equality was implicit in the Constitution and that the courts would ultimately affirm it. It requested interested groups to take steps that would lead to a ruling to that effect. As for the ERA, the subcommittee recommended a statement for the commission: "In view of the promise of this constitutional approach, the Commission at this time takes no position on the proposed equal rights amendment". The recommendation carefully refrained from criticising the efforts of any group with regard to improving the status of women, remarking that the progress women had made in the recent past was due to the work of civic and women's groups; the statement urged that such activities continue. The subcommittee proposal went on: "[The Commission] therefore commends and encourages the continued efforts of such interested groups in educating the public to the problems and in urging action within the . . . government to the end that full partnership of women may become a reality whether effected by federal or state legislation . . . or through appropriate federal or state constitutional Amendment, or by test litigation within the existing constitutional framework". Marguerite Rawalt was deeply relieved at the recommendation.

At the meeting of April 5, the committee changed the recommendation from "at this time takes no position on the proposed equal rights amendment" to "does not take a position in favour of the equal rights amendment at this time". The majority of the committee opposed the ERA and felt obliged to say so. But those who objected to the constitutional amendment believed they were leaving options open, both by including the phrase *at this time* and by encouraging other groups to work toward the end they considered most suitable, even including a constitutional amendment. In making this statement, the committee hoped to placate ERA supporters.

The commission was not at first so cautious or so diplomatic. Far more than the committee, it seemed willing to turn the amendment down flat. Marguerite Rawalt chaired the discussion at the commission meeting of April 23–24; the long ERA supporter, she had more at stake than any other commission member. Carefully she explained to the commission the reasoning behind the committee's delicately worded recommendation and its desire not to bar any course of action. John Macy, chairman of the Civil Service Commission, was not persuaded. Unwilling to admit even the possibility of supporting the ERA, he contended: "You weaken the basic position . . . if you also continue to ride the equal rights amendment horse." Rawalt tried to persuade the commission against complete rejection of the ERA, saying it was a national commission's duty to encourage rather than to foreclose action, and she cited the support of the BPW and the General Federation of Women's Clubs and of Presidents Truman, Eisenhower, and, ironically, Kennedy for the ERA. On the other side, both Henry David, president of the New School for Social Research, and Viola Hymes, president of the National Council of Jewish Women, argued against hedging, including phrases like *at the present time*.

They insisted that because the president's commission was to go out of existence in October, it could either endorse the amendment or reject it, but it could not suggest that the position might change in the future. Caroline Ware, herself a victim of sex discrimination, dissented. She suggested that if the Court refused to rule favourably in a test case, some constitutional amendment might be appropriate. Although David and Hymes repeatedly asked for a clear commission vote on the subject, vice-chairman Richard Lester, Caroline Ware, and Mary Bunting, the president of Radcliffe, seemed eager to avoid one. Ware suggested that a "pro or con" approach was "wrong" in view of Murray's new suggestion. Rawalt, who recognised the certainty of a rejection if a poll were taken, predicted that a "yea or nay" vote would result in a newspaper headline the commission might wish to avoid. The majority of the commission appeared sensitive to the prospective enmity a flat denunciation of the ERA would bring from the BPW and other pro-ERA women's groups: only three voted in favour of a substitute statement offered by Henry David and Norman Nicholson of Kaiser Industries clearly condemning the amendment.

A substitute drafted by the Department of Justice that did not change the substance of the committee draft won greater favour. It read: "In view of the fact that a constitutional Amendment does not appear to be necessary to establish the principle of equality, the Commission believes that constitutional changes should not be sought unless, at some future time, it appears from court decisions that a need for such action exists". Rawalt objected to the contention of "fact" in the first part of the recommendation, and the commission eliminated that part and substituted the word *since:* "Since a constitutional Amendment does not appear to be necessary. . . ." ERA opponents then maintained that the word *since* indicated that they were not foreclosing the possibility that the amendment might become desirable under unforeseen future circumstances; they therefore moved to strike the words after *sought*. Despite Rawalt's objection, the motion carried ten to five. Rawalt, who felt sorely defeated, asked to be recorded in opposition. The other four votes opposed are unknown.

On the day following the vote, Rawalt made a final attempt to modify the commission statement. She observed that deleting the words from the Justice Department recommendation—"unless at some future time it appears from court decisions that a need for such action exists"—appeared to close off the consideration of amendments in the future. Rawalt argued that many had said that the word *since* indicated a recognition that a constitutional amendment might be appropriate if the Murray approach failed, and that this position could be stated more clearly by inserting the word *now*—"the Commission believes that constitutional changes should not now be sought". Henry David, although an enemy of the ERA, seemed eager for some sort of compromise and suggested "need not now be sought", a change Rawalt quickly accepted. Margaret Mealey of the National Council of Catholic Women, another strong ERA opponent, seconded the motion. The motion carried, but the vote was not recorded, except that Henry David asked to be noted as "not voting". Rawalt had succeeded in averting a flat denunciation of the ERA.

But more important, despite lingering concern that even the Fourteenth Amendment approach might imperil some legislation commission members thought valuable, the commission had followed the committee recommendation and asserted that women had to have some affirmation of their rights to equal treatment under the Fourteenth Amendment to the Constitution. Coming from a citadel of the Women's Bureau coalition, it was the first genuine move toward compromise since the NWP had proposed exempting protective laws from the ERA forty years before.

Equality of Rights: "Basic to Democracy"

In its report the President's Commission on the Status of Women emphasised its stand that women needed the protection of the Constitution against arbitrary sex discrimination; it did not stress its position on the ERA. The section of the report entitled "Women Under the Law" began with the statement that "equality of rights under the law for all persons, male or female, is so basic to democracy . . . that it must be reflected in the fundamental law of the land." It went on to say that whereas the commission believed that this principle was already incorporated in the Fifth and Fourteenth Amendments to the Constitution, but that some state laws made distinctions between men and women that "do not appear to be reasonable in the light of the multiple activities of women in present-day society." The commission had considered three approaches to dealing with such laws, it said: test litigation looking toward Supreme Court review, the Equal Rights Amendment, and state legislative action. The report continued: "Since the Commission is convinced that the U.S. Constitution now embodies equality of rights for men and women, we conclude that a constitutional amendment need not now be sought in order to establish this principle. But judicial clarification is imperative in order that remaining ambiguities with respect to the constitutional protection of women's rights be eliminated". Interested groups should, the commission said, seek appropriate test cases. In addition, the commission asked all branches of government to "scrutinise" their laws and to remove "archaic" discriminatory standards. With respect to the activity of other groups the commission "commended" and "encouraged" education and action "to the end that full equality of rights may become a reality". No specific proposals were mentioned.

On the day the commission report came out, Peterson wrote to Senator Carl Hayden to thank him for his efforts in staving off the Equal Rights Amendment. His rider, she said, had constituted "an indispensable safeguard." She expressed her hope that "active work on the ERA could be deferred to allow a reasonable opportunity for testing the effectiveness of the new approach recommended by the Commission"; she was sure, she told him, that the Supreme Court would uphold protective laws for women under the commission plan. She asked him, however, to be sure to continue appending his rider if the ERA were introduced.

Predictably, the National Woman's party opposed the commission's conclusion with respect to the ERA. "In our opinion", explained an NWP statement, "the fate of American women should not be left to a possible future change in the attitude of the Supreme Court". The NWP did not object philosophically to the proposed reinterpretation of the constitution; it avowed only that the possibility was unlikely. "Such a change", the party declared, "might not come for years, or it might never come". In any case, the party expressed the hope that the president's commission would signal the end of the study of women's status, which had been investigated ever since the presentation of the first colonial petition for women's suffrage 315 years before. Adoption of the "simple, clear and comprehensive" equal Rights Amendment constituted the next logical step, the party maintained. Privately, Emma Guffey Miller called the outcome " a contradictory report from a packed committee. Alice Paul proposed that the NWP simply ignore the commission report and go forward with the ERA, which again awaited action in both the Senate and the House.

Congressional opponents, however, believed that the proposal of the president's commission eliminated whatever chance the ERA had in Congress. Carl Hayden sent copies of the commission report to correspondents, telling them: "In view of the recommendations . . . , I doubt that it would be possible to obtain two-thirds majority in each branch of the Congress in favour of submitting the Equal Rights Amendment for ratification by three-fourths of the State Legislatures". He suggested that persons who complained of discrimination file federal suits.

Peterson herself viewed the commission suggestion on constitutional equality as a constructive plan of action, and she called a meeting ten days after the commission presented its report to discuss its implementation. She invited the National Woman's party to attend, and three representatives, including

Alice Paul, participated, along with delegates from several other women's groups. Although Paul publicly expressed her hope and support for legal appeals through the courts, she continued to believe that such a strategy would "cripple the movement for the Equal Rights Amendment", which she did not intend to allow. An expanded meeting of organisations willing to work on the Fourteenth Amendment approach took place two weeks later, with some seventeen groups present, including, again, the National Woman's party, which wanted to monitor the proceedings. The group elected the BPW president to chair a clearinghouse for the dissemination of information, creating much the same structure as the National Committee on Equal Pay. Plans were made for future meetings. Despite the uncertainty of the outcome, and the ambivalence of the NWP, for the first time since the introduction of the ERA in 1923 women's organisations on both sides of the question were uniting to work on an alternative plan for constitutional equality.

The creation of the President's Commission on the Status of Women thus succeeded in achieving one of the goals of the Women's Bureau coalition. During the commission's life it forestalled action on the ERA in Congress, and it developed an alternative that seemed likely to sap the strength of the amendment's appeal in the future.

But by agreeing that women needed to be considered "equal under law," it broke the long-standing stalemate that had hobbled concerted action on behalf of American women since the end of World War II. The President's Commission on the Status of Women had included the amendment's backers; it had further declined either to make an unacceptable policy statement at its inception or permanently to reject the amendment at the commission's conclusion. In fact, the commission's suggested alternative—"that the principle of equality [for women] become firmly established in constitutional doctrine" by means of an "early and definitive Supreme Court pronouncement"—was acceptable ideologically to the ERA's advocates; most merely thought it impractical. Moreover, the amendment's opponents had even suggested that constitutional amendment might be required if the judiciary did not vindicate their belief in the Fifth and Fourteenth Amendments. The central argument over the ERA had now been sidestepped in such a way that both proponents and opponents could work together on constitutional equality and other women's issues as well. Although the NWP doubted that the Supreme Court would ever rule in favour of equal rights for women, other ERA advocates contended that a well-organised case had not before been presented, and they were willing, at least for a time, to take on the task.

The outcome of the Commission's work on this issue thus proved salutary; the way in which the commission functioned had an equally useful result. By isolating the discussion of the ERA during its life, the President's Commission on the Status of Women found itself able to embark on what it viewed as its main work: the creation of a programme for women that would address the many problems that constitutional equality would not rectify.

6

A Unified Agenda for Women's Rights

By the 1960s, the political objective of equal treatment for women seemed more within reach than it had in the previous postwar years. The ambivalence over new social roles for women had abated as the family and the economy revealed not only the ability to tolerate women as permanent workers but also the need for women to assume this role. A president now held office who was committed to growth and the liberal agenda of government intervention on behalf of the social good. The internal politics of the Kennedy administration had given a particular shape to the development of a strategy of which the President's Commission on the Status of Women was the centrepiece. Sequestering the ERA allowed the commission to move toward developing a unified agenda to expand opportunities for women.

As soon as the commission inquiry began, however, it became apparent that it would not resolve the philosophic contradiction that had beset all previous efforts to improve women's opportunities outside the home. The commission took the stand that women had the right to be full-time permanent workers and to be treated as such according to their merits, but only so long as their traditional relationship to their children remained unchanged. As far as the commission was concerned, women's obligation to be the primary nurturers of children remained immutable, a critical difference between men and women as workers. This fundamental conflict between equal opportunity for women in the public realm and fulfilment of the role of traditional motherhood showed itself in the ambivalence that pervaded the commission's discussion and reports.

The inherent incongruity left the commission open to criticism from both sides. The executive order establishing the commission stressed employment aspects of women's status, reflecting the new social acceptance of women as workers. It charged the commission with "developing recommendations for overcoming discriminations in government and private employment on the basis of sex and . . . developing recommendations for services which will enable women to continue their roles as wives and mothers while making a maximum contribution to the world around them". Because of the emphasis on work problems, some accused the commission of urging mothers to leave their children and join the labour force. Following Eleanor Roosevelt's discussion of the PSCW with the president on her television show, "Prospects of making", Lee Udall, wife of the secretary of the interior and the mother of six children, told a *Washington Post* reporter that the programme "didn't do a thing to elevate the profession of motherhood". Letters to the president from the public made the same point. In response, Peterson drafted a reply affirming her conviction that motherhood was the "major role of the American woman" and her "primary responsibility". Conscious indeed of the national commitment to women as mothers, whenever the commission encountered a conflict between the roles of mother and of workers, it usually endorsed the former at the expense of the latter.

Because it supported the general view that sex roles could not fundamentally change, the commission could not reconcile the underlying contradiction between its affirmation of motherhood and the simultaneous assertion that women shared with men "the freedom to choose among different life patterns." Hyman Bookbinder, who represented the secretary of commerce on the commission, observed: "It is a fact of life—past, present, and future—that the great majority of women either choose to, or have to, devote their energies and their talents to the rearing of children and the management of homelife during at least half of their adult years". The implication of this "fact of life" for Bookbinder followed: "We should not pretend that women as a group are equal to men as a group in qualifying for participation in the world of work and in public affairs". Margaret Mealey, speaking for the National Council of Catholic Women, of which she was executive director, cautioned that women's nature and the well-being of her family imposed limitations on her public life. The Committee on Home and Community maintained in its report: "Over and above whatever role modern women play in the community . . . , the care of the home and the children remains their unique responsibility. No matter how much everyday tasks are shared or how equal the marriage partnership may be, the care of the children is primarily the province of the mother. This is not debatable as a philosophy. It is and will remain a fact of life." Logically, the commission also espoused a corollary belief, that the major responsibility for the family's financial support fell to the father. Given these assumptions and a stated objective of equal opportunity for working women, vice-chairman Richard Lester pointed out to the commission that it had a problem of "inconsistent justification for . . . different recommendations". The dichotomy between the primacy of traditional sex roles and the goal of equal treatment for women at work produced a tension which the commission never satisfactorily explored or resolved. No coherent intellectual argument for women's equal treatment would emerge from the president's commission.

Not only were the commission's choices limited by its unwillingness to question the sex-role structure or prevailing beliefs about the nature of women in American society, but the commission's desire to recommend proposals that would likely be endorsed by the administration, adopted, and implemented also constrained its options. Because it coveted widespread approval, the commission rejected most potentially contentious positions, from fundamental changes in the Social Security system to endorsement of the provision of birth control information. It did not intend to begin a debate over the basic principles that sustained the social order. Hyman Bookbinder pointed out facetiously that if the commission took the position that monogamy, for example, created certain problems, the publicity directed to that opinion would overwhelm all the other material in the report and cause the public to dismiss the balance of the recommendations. Convinced that even internal dissension would vitiate the strength of the suggestions, the commission also pursued unanimity, sometimes sacrificing a majority opinion to achieve it. Both the committees and the full commission strove to produce documents acceptable to the administration, to which end Esther Peterson cleared all proposals and reports with cabinet and White House officials before their release. The President's Commission on the Status of Women very much represented a mainstream reform attempt, working for the Kennedy administration within the constraints of prevailing values and liberal politics.

Because they were working within a liberal consensus, most commission members felt no need even to articulate the principles they herd in common. Commission recommendations evinced a faith in the ability to make meaningful changes without radically altering the economic or political structure. With constructive leadership, the commissioners behaved, the nation progressed through time toward increasing freedom and greater equality of opportunity, to the benefit of both individuals and the society as a whole. Therefore, the commission assumed, government had the right and the duty, using "expert advice," to intervene within the private sector in order to bring about desirable goals, provide services, and assist those in need. Few of the commissioners found it necessary to define their terms, although many would no doubt have differed as to what constituted appropriate federal intervention in either the private sector or the family.

No commission member grappled with the idea that business might find a marginal female labour force efficient and economical; instead, recommendations contended that better opportunities for women would inevitably result in larger profits and increasing productivity. Many did acknowledge that women should not individually have to bear all the costs of childrearing—that industry and educational institutions should seek some accommodation to the wants of women and children. But none suggested that maternity and childrearing ranked first, with employment structured to suit those needs. With certain modifications, women would will have to fit into a male-designed world.

Within its ideological and political boundaries, however, the commission made a conscientious effort to establish as expeditiously as possible a record of responsible action on behalf of women, both in the home and at work. Recommendations took note of differences in class, race, political ideology, and individual preferences, as well as some social norms it deemed inappropriate to support. The total package of recommendations resulted in a blueprint for change that, if implemented, would significantly enlarge the range of choices for American women.

Federal Employment

The president's commission began its operations by addressing employment discrimination practiced by the federal government—the obvious place to start. The nation's largest employer, it had sixty thousand women on its payroll. Moreover, the government practiced a blatant form of sex discrimination: agency heads by law could limit jobs to persons of one sex or the other. Taking steps against sex discrimination in the civil service presented few procedural problems and, because the form of discrimination was so bald, few ideological problems.

Sex discrimination in the civil service had a long history. The first women clerks had been hired specifically to provide cheap labour. In 1864 Congress enacted a law allowing the appointment of female clerks at a rate of six hundred dollars per year, half the lowest government wage. By 1870, however, with more than seven hundred women employed in federal offices in Washington, Congress passed a new provision permitting department heads to hire women to fill the regular clerkship grades and to pay them the commensurate salary. In the revised statutes, adopted the following year, this section came to read: "Women may, in the discretion of the head of any department, be appointed to any clerkship therein authorised by law, upon the same . . . conditions . . . as are prescribed for men". Although clearly intended as an authority to pay women the same rate as male clerks, the Civil Service Commission (CSC) interpreted the provision to mean that Congress had granted agency heads the absolute right to specify the preferred sex of a worker for any job. Agency heads used their prerogative almost invariably to select women for the low-paying jobs and men for the more responsible ones. In 1919 only 5 percent of new women federal employees received salaries over $1,299, compared to 46 percent of the men. Under pressure from the Women's Bureau coalition, the CSC that year had rescinded the rule barring women from more than 60 percent of the civil service examinations, but it maintained the right of agency heads to designate sex in requesting names from the eligibles list for employment. In 1923 the Classification Act mandated equal pay for equal work regardless of sex, but the right of federal managers to hire by sex was not addressed. Finally, in 1932, just before his term was to expire, President Herbert Hoover, acting on the advice of Republican members of the National Woman's party, issued an executive order rescinding the right of agency heads to select by sex, although reserving the right to the Civil Service Commission in the case of jobs where sex represented a bona fide occupational qualification.

Although this decision pleased the National Woman's party,

the Women's Bureau coalition had mixed feelings. Before the passage of the Veterans' Preference Act during the Harding administration, they too had argued for the change. But because veterans had points added to their scores automatically, women had less chance of falling among the top three eligibles from which appointments were customarily made. Therefore, the Women's Bureau preferred selection by sex, which at least gave women access to clerical positions and permitted sympathetic agency heads, like Mary Anderson, to choose women regardless of the availability of men with higher scores. The interests of each side reflected its class orientation. The NWP sought to open opportunities so that able women could move into upper-level jobs; the Women's Bureau concerned itself with the right of women to entry-level positions.

Soon after FDR became president, the Women's Bureau gained enough leverage to assure the outcome it sought. The bureau pointed out that under Hoover's executive order, appointments of women to the civil service did actually decline (although the Depression, which impelled all employers to give preference to men, probably accounted for the change at least as much). Mary Anderson asked the new president to countermand Hoover's instructions. In response, the Civil Service Commission polled women's organisations throughout the country; with six replies in favour of restoring the previous rule and two preferring the new one, Roosevelt's attorney general ruled that Hoover's executive order had been illegal. Only Congress, he said, could rescind the power it had given agency heads to select by sex. In October 1934, to the NWP's disgust, Franklin Roosevelt reversed Hoover's directive.

The policy remained in force throughout the forties and fifties, although it had become increasingly apparent that, veterans preference or no, selection by sex consigned women to low-level jobs. In 1954 the median grade for women had been four; for men, seven (excluding postal employees). Out of every hundred women federal workers, 80 percent held jobs in grades one to five, compared to only 25 percent of the men; less than 1 per cent of women served as administrators, as opposed to 9 per cent of males. By 1959, the median for men had risen by two grades but remained at GS-4 for women; half of all women were found in the four lowest grades, compared with only one fifth of the men. Even in professional positions, the median grade for women was lower than for men generally, GS-7 compared to GS-9.

Despite these facts, repeated presidential statements about the need for women in policy-making positions, and the increasing disapproval of women's organisations, neither the Democratic nor the Republican administrations of these decades took steps to limit the right of federal managers to select by sex. Complaints and appeals to the CSC and the attorney general brought the response that only Congress could revoke this authority. But when, in 1957, Representative Marguerite Stitt Church (R-Ill.) introduced a bill to amend section 165 of the Revised Statutes to remove the discretion in appointments, the Civil Service Commission reacted unenthusiastically, and the bill died in committee.

The CSC had not deemed the status of women federal employees a problem. Although a 1959 federal employment survey had found that women, still one-quarter of the federal labour force, continued to be clustered in the lowest grades, the commission failed to identify discrimination as a cause of this situation. After all, it noted, more men than women were trained professionals and therefore were naturally classified in the higher grades. Yet the Commission did concede that even in fields such as social administration, which contained as many women as men, the median grade for men was still GS-13, and that for women was GS-12. The commission suggested that still another factor might account for the disparity: the traditional employment pattern of women. Because women left the labour force to raise children, the "interruption of their careers retards their progress up the promotion ladder". Nevertheless, the commission cheerfully observed, there was still room for women at the top. Out of 575,990 women federal employees, 18 had attained positions among the 1,496 employees in grades sixteen, seventeen, and eighteen, slightly over 1 percent.

In seeking to eliminate so obvious a form of sex discrimination within the civil service, the President's Commission on the Status of Women did not need to address the conflict between motherhood and equal opportunities at work, and in the presence of the Civil Service Commission it did not have to draw up formal rules regarding penalties or affirmative action. In addition, John Kennedy was already on record favouring the eradication of sex bias in the civil service. When he announced the creation of the presidential commission, Kennedy (with prompting from Peterson, Senator Philip Hart [D-Mich.], and others) had expressed his belief that the federal career service should be a "showcase" of equal opportunity in employment. He at that time instructed John Macy, chairman of the Civil Service Commission, to review policies and procedures to ensure that selection was made solely on merit without regard to sex. As president, Kennedy could execute additional PSCW recommendations on the subject without further ado.

The PCSW promptly recommended the policy change and John Kennedy promptly implemented it. Robert Kennedy reversed the ruling made by Roosevelt's attorney general, and the president put CSC chief John Macy in charge of eliminating the discriminatory practice of selecting personnel by sex. "Bona fide occupational qualification" exceptions would be few.

Merely forbidding agency heads from excluding women did not mean that more women would be hired, and no one considered penalising executives who did not place women in upper-level jobs; nevertheless, change was visible as early as a year later. Many agencies had appointed women to particular positions for the first time, and the CSC had instituted monitoring procedures. Although the configuration of employment did not change at once the idea of equal opportunity for women in employment had been introduced, confirmed, and legitimated.

The president's commission also addressed, albeit cautiously, the other form of federal employment of women: presidential appointments. Although no woman representative of the Democratic National Committee sat on the commission (a fact that irritated many DNC members), the PCSW nevertheless recognised administration appointments as being worthy of attention. Still, criticism of the administration would be impolitic, so the members decided to focus on the needs for the future rather than the failures of the past. The commission's recommendation on nominations read: "Increasing consideration should continually be given to the appointment of women of demonstrated ability and political sensitivity to policy-making positions". The White House did not find the suggestion objectionable, and Dan Fenn, head of the administration's "Talent Search", met with Margaret Hickey, chairman of the commission's Committee on Federal Employment, to find a way to implement it. Fenn deplored the practice of merely supplying lists of names of women seeking positions. He therefore proposed a small committee of women who would help locate the right woman for a given job and lobby to appoint her—in short, that the president's commission perform the function India Edwards had fulfilled for Truman. But because the commission had less than one year to its conclusion, it could not assume such a responsibility. Kennedy's appointment record remained undistinguished.

Private Employment

The desire to make the civil service a "showcase" reflected in part the presidential commission's belief that private employers would emulate the federal model. But if the federal government intended to take action with regard to sex discrimination in the private sector, the guidelines of enforcement and consequences of noncompliance had to be spelled out more clearly than for the civil service, where the Civil Service Commission could implement a general policy on an *ad hoc* basis.

Both political and philosophical considerations, however,

prevented the commission from seeking to penalise business for sex discrimination. James Roosevelt (D-Calif.) proposed a fair employment practice bill in 1962 that barred discrimination based on sex as well as on race, but the NAACP and the Departments of Justice and Labour objected to including women in the bill. The House Committee on Education and Labour omitted the sex provision on the motion of Edith Green (D-Oreg.) in order to give the president's commission time to study the best methods of achieving employment equity for women. Neither the PCSW's Committee on Private Employment nor the commission as a whole believed that coercive measures would win acceptance from either the business community or Congress. In addition, because no sanctions against sex bias obtained within the federal government, it would be hard to defend punitive measures against private business for the same offense. More to the point, although they held up equal treatment as ideal, both the committee on Private Employment and the commission, reflecting the beliefs of most Americans, regarded differential treatment in employment on the basis of sex warranted under some circumstances because of women's familial obligations.

By the time the commission began to consider the attitude of business toward women, the administration had already taken executive action with respect to racial discrimination in private employment. Shortly after assuming office, John Kennedy had issued an executive order (EO 10925) establishing the President's Committee on Equal Employment Opportunity. The order required federal contractors to agree not to discriminate on the basis of "race, creed, colour or national origin" and to take affirmative action to ensure equal treatment. A second executive order, issued in June 1963, extended the initial provision to federally assisted programmes receiving grants, loans, insurance, or guarantees. The possibility of including "sex" in EO 10925 had been considered, but administration drafters concluded that racial discrimination constituted enough of a burden without adding other conditions, such as sex, age, or handicap. Moreover, ever since World War II a widespread social movement to end racial discrimination had been pressuring the government and seeking to change public attitudes—and with some success: race had become less and less a legitimate criterion for discrimination. Neither a social movement nor a coherent feminist philosophy existed to support the inclusion of a prohibition on sex-based discrimination in an executive order (or a bill, also considered) to ban racial bias in private employment.

The president's commission considered this issue a fertile field for policy initiatives, and, although sex discrimination had been omitted from the first executive order, the commission continued to view the relationship between the federal government and its contractors as the most accessible vehicle for bringing about some change in the private sector. The president could prohibit sex discrimination merely by fiat, and an executive order pertaining to contractors would protect a significant number of workers. In 1960, the federal government bought about 20 percent of all goods and services produced in the country, and the one hundred largest defense contractors employed ten million workers.

The question for the Committee on Private Employment to resolve centred on the kind of executive order to recommend. Committee member Caroline Davis, director of the Women's Division of the United Automobile Workers, strongly urged that the president ban discrimination based on sex and include penalties and machinery for enforcement. She had supported the addition of the word *sex* to EO 10925, and because of her defeat on this issue, she said, she had failed to win a prohibition against sex discrimination in the automobile industry contracts of 1961.

The Private Employment Committee refused to go along with her proposal, though. As committee chairman Richard Lester explained, "There are very good grounds, apparently, for discrimination against women in connection with training, promotion and upgrading in certain lines". Because women differed from men in motivation and career aspirations, and usually interrupted their work lives to raise families, the government, Lester contended, would find it difficult "to determine the line between justified and unjustified selection of males over against females in training and promotion". Moreover, said Lester, because illegitimate sex discrimination could not at that point be specified, any executive order prohibiting it would have to depend for enforcement on "moral suasion and company consultation". The experience gained using these techniques would, he argued, permit the formulation of stronger measures later if they proved necessary.

The administration stepped in to quell the dispute. The new secretary of labour, Willard Wirtz, refused to endorse an executive order that relied on more than education and moral suasion for its enforcement. At its meeting one week later, the Committee on Private Employment, in keeping with the administration's wishes, passed a recommendation for a contract clause to be specified in an executive order: "It is the policy of the Government that there should be no discrimination against women in regard to hiring, training or promotion in employment by reason of their sex. In the performance of this contract, the contractor is requested to use his best efforts to comply with this policy in order to assure that equal employment practices for women are observed." After strenuous objections from Caroline Davis and Muriel Ferris, Senator Philip Hart's legislative assistant, the committee compromised and changed *is requested to* to *shall*.

In its report, the committee recounted its reasons for not recommending the amendment of EO 10925 and for preferring persuasion to compulsion. "The consensus," the report explained, "was that the nature of discrimination on the basis of sex and the reasons for it are so different [from race] that a separate programme is necessary to eliminate barriers to the employment and advancement of women". Volunteerism would permit business managers to demonstrate that they could act without coercion, and a no coercive programme would therefore elicit more support from industry, Congress, and other groups, the committee asserted. Information could be collected "in a cooperative atmosphere" that would permit distinguishing "differentiation that is justifiable on the basis of sex from differentiation that cannot be justified". In cases of wilful noncompliance, firms could conceivably be barred from federal contracts, and if more definite penalities turned out to be necessary they could be added later. Only Caroline Ware dissented, citing experience with voluntary compliance and cases of racial discrimination.

The commission would not accept Davis's proposal to add the word *sex* to EO 10925, which it believed meant ignoring the impact of family responsibilities on women workers and their employers, nor could it envision forcing private employers to share with women the costs of taking time out from work to raise families. Thus, despite initial protestations of the commission's planners that "prevailing institutions and work practices . . . largely shaped by and for men" limited women's chances, the commission did not propose to forbid sex discrimination. Unable to reconcile the conflict between pursuit of equality for women and endorsement of the traditional obligations of women, the commission suggested that women's interrupted work patterns might justify exclusion from on-the-job development programmes—implying that women would have to continue to pay the price of lost promotions and missed wage increases for fulfilling what the commission deemed to be their appropriate roles. Further, PCSW personnel viewed with sympathy the objections of civil servants and business people who did not want to be saddled with additional burdens in getting or offering contracts for government supplies. Finally, the commission did not want to place the White House in a position where it would refuse to comply with a PSCW recommendation. The commission had been designed to enhance the president's reputation, not embarrass him. Given the nature of the dispute, political considerations dictated leaving the recommendation vague. Interested in achieving widespread endorsement of its vies, the commission, in this instance as in others, attempted to arrive at positions that would not unduly inconvenience its constituents, even at the expense of working women's opportunities. It thus wound up in large measure mirroring rather than advancing the state of national opinion.

Although hardly a battle cry, the commission's statement denouncing discrimination in employment still advanced the cause of wider opportunities for women. In its report the commission called attention to the number of women employed (one worker in every three was female) and the need for their skills and their income. It also decried women's low wages and countered the myths, such as increased absenteeism, that employers offered to justify discrimination. "Reluctance to consider women applicants on their merits," the commission declared, "results in underutilisation of capacities that the economy needs and stunts the development of higher skills". The commission enunciated for the first time a federal policy censuring discrimination against women in employment by the federal government itself, by the private sector, and by state governments receiving federal grants. Although the limits to discrimination were not clearly drawn, at least, according to the commission, there ought to be some limits.

Protective Labour Legislation

The commission could not easily insist on full equality for women in hiring and training, but it was able to come closer to affirming nondiscriminatory treatment for women under protective labour laws, the coverage of which could be extended to men rather than withdrawn from women.

Because employers had always used labour laws to justify discrimination, advocates of the Equal Rights Amendment had for a long time urged that such legislation either apply to men as well as women or be eliminated. The Women's Bureau, in contrast, had traditionally maintained that protective labour laws helped the overwhelming majority of women and hurt only a few. When faced with the imminent threat of the ERA, advocates of protective labour legislation, fearing that the amendment would result not in extension but in obliteration of the labour laws, fought the amendment vigorously and defended the laws for women. With the Committee on Civil and Political Rights working on a method for achieving constitutional equality while still safeguarding protective laws for women, the Committee on Protective Labour Legislation was free to consider the laws themselves, undisturbed by the heated ERA controversy. By the 1960s many of those most committed to protective labour laws were willing to acknowledge that some of the more restrictive and rigid rules did more harm than good. It was up to the Committee on Protective Labour Legislation to determine the difference between the laws still useful and those now antiquated and to find a way to reconcile the demand for equal opportunity for women and the expectation of special protection.

Consideration of the laws apart from the Equal Rights Amendment produced a ready accord; in most cases the Committee on Protective Labour Legislation, and the commission as a whole, concurred in principle with ERA proponents. The most desirable outcome, committee members concluded, was the extension to men of the laws in effect protecting women. However, whereas ERA adherents saw constitutional equality as causing the beneficial changes in state laws, the Committee on Protective Labour Legislation strongly believed that laws pertaining to women should remain in force until they were superseded by better laws covering men as well.

This judgement did not present any problems for the committee in most areas of discussion, which were quickly decided by consensus. At the first meeting, members endorsed the extension of minimum wage legislation with premium pay for overtime at both federal and state levels to men and women workers presently uncovered; likewise for equal pay legislation. The committee also agreed that industrial homework should be eliminated. Later the committee voted in favour of a flexible weight-lifting law pertaining to both men and women. Cash maternity benefits under disability programmes and the right to maternity leave also met with approval.

The sticking point came over hours legislation. Most members concurred that state law should establish an absolute number of hours for workers, but committee member Henry David, a prominent labour historian, adamantly and successfully resisted a proposal to recommend extending prohibitions on women's hours to male workers. He contended both that the PCSW had no mandate to recommend laws for men and that proposing a limit to the number of hours men could work would elicit "howls of rage". Furthermore, David argued, hours laws for women were well established; applying them to men would raise "a whole new series of questions which we certainly are not able to deal with and on which we have seen no basic data at all". Ultimately, after David's vehement argument, the committee recommended that hours laws set a definite maximum for women, that they be administered "flexibly," and that women in administrative, executive, and professional jobs be exempted.

Commission members greeted the committee recommendation with varying degrees of satisfaction. Margaret Hickey said she had hoped the time had come to apply these standards equally to men. Henry David explained to her the reasoning of the committee—which was in fact his own—that hours laws for men would not gain public acceptance. Hickey responded that such a consideration did not appear to be a very good reason to burden women. Many commission members, including Peterson, expressed the view that overtime pay as a deterrent might be preferable to maximums, but David argued strongly for his position, insisting that the commission was making trouble for itself on the matter and that to come out against maximum hours for women would be breaking with "a body of history which meant something and conceivably still does mean something". Sarcastically, he admitted that the original resolution did have a weakness; it was, he said, "realistic".

Faced with an apparent deadlock, Peterson had a statement drawn up before the next meeting detailing the Department of Labour's position on the issue. According to this position paper, the department desired adequate labour standards for all workers, and it judged premium pay for additional hours for both men and women as the best way to shorten the workday. The Department concluded that, where special hours laws for women represented the best attainable protection at present, they should be "maintained, strengthened and expanded". The commission adopted this position almost verbatim adding the exemption of professional and executive women from the committee's original recommendation. Although David believed that the commission had adopted his position, this statement differed in that it spoke of maximum hours laws only as interim measures, to be eliminated when states enacted laws requiring premium pay for overtime. Hours laws constituted the only area of conflict with respect to protective labour legislation and, except for pregnancy and maternity leave, became the only kind of labour legislation about which the committee and the commission proposed differential treatment of women workers—and even this remaining distinction was to be temporary. The gap between the Women's Bureau coalition and proponents of the ERA was growing smaller.

Taken all together, the commission's proposals on employment revealed its ambivalence toward women's roles. While continuing to endorse equality in the civil service, in private employment, and in labour law, the commission also spoke of "justifiable" discrimination and extending and strengthening hours laws for women. Recognising that private employers were unlikely to change their behaviour without federal direction, it nevertheless declined to specify the action the White House should take. Because it was caught between the fundamentally contradictory ideals of traditional womanhood and equality, the commission could not make a clear statement.

Education

The dichotomy of women's needing both equal and different treatment that ran through the commission's discussions on employment also weighed on the consideration of recommendations concerning education. The commission maintained that educational institutions needed to accommodate to the patterns of women's lives so that women who followed traditional paths could reenter the labour force when their children had grown. Educational programmes had to be available in the community, through either local junior colleges or correspondence schools. Schools had a responsibility to offer part-time study, financial aid, and flexible academic and residency requirements.

But the educational establishment had another obligation as well. According to both the Committee on Education and the commission as a whole, educational institutions needed to help women prepare for their special role. "The expectation that a woman will become a wife and mother differentiates the educational requirements of girl and boy from the very beginning," the committee report asserted. The commission cautioned that "widening the choice for women beyond their doorstep does not imply neglect of their education for responsibilities in the home". All girls and women should learn about childcare and family relations, nutrition, family finances, and "the relation of individuals and families to society". The commission did not recommend such a programme for boys and men.

Yet at the same time that the commission proposed educational programmes to fortify prevailing sex roles, it also argued that education played a key role in expanding women's horizons. Counselling women, the commission contended, required special skills: "From infancy, roles held up to girls deflect talents into narrow channels . . . . Imaginative counselling can lift aspirations beyond stubbornly persistent assumptions about 'women's roles' and 'women's interests' and result in choices that have inner authenticity for their makers". But here again, the commission refused to acknowledge the underlying problem. Many of the characteristically male-dominated fields did not mesh well with the traditional roles of women. If childcare remained ultimately a female responsibility, as the commission assumed it should, fewer women could be expected to overcome the hurdles in fulfilling both the role of nurturer and that of career professional. A young woman who received both the homemaking education the commission prescribed and counselling to become a mechanical engineer had to sort out conflicting messages. Its recommendations on both employment and education disclosed the commission's vacillation between the two ideals it professed.

Financial Security

When it came to issues of family support, however, the traditional view of women as dependent ultimately took clear precedence. Consonant with its view that women had unique responsibilities with respect to families which justified differential treatment in employment, the commission also affirmed that men had to continue to fulfil traditional support obligations. The Committee on Civil and Political Rights recommended that "in view of the childbearing and homemaking functions of the wife" the husband should continue to bear the primary burden of financial support. The commission concurred in the committee's judgement, which coloured many of the commission's additional suggestions.

The Commission made no recommendation for changes in the Social Security system for women workers who paid Social Security taxes and, in many cases, received no additional awards over that which they would have gotten as wives who had not made payments. The system presumed the dependency of both wives and children on male workers and so also denied benefits even for the children of working women. The commission did, however, emphasise the need for increased payments to the widows of workers and to divorced women.

Part of the commission's reluctance to tackle these questions came from the complexity of the Social Security system and the expense of making changes in benefits. But the Committee on Social Insurance and Taxes went out of its way to affirm that it would not "be appropriate for the social insurance programme to provide a benefit so that the father could stay at home to care for the child" in the event of the mother's death. Childcare, after all, was women's work. Thus, despite the assertion throughout the commission report that women worked to provide necessities for their families, the commission nevertheless failed to acknowledge that such families would continue to need the mother's income if she died—without recognising that this omission undercut its initial premise.

Although the commission declined to explore the implications for equality in employment of leaving traditional assumptions about financial support untouched it did acknowledge some danger in the complete economic dependency of the homemaker. Most states followed the common-law precept that income belonged to the person who earned it. Thus, in a family where the husband worked for pay and the wife did not, she had no legal right to any of the family income or property. The commission took exception to this state of affairs. Calling marriage a partnership "in which each spouse makes a different but equally important contribution," it asserted that wives should have a "legally defined substantial right in the earnings" of the husband and in the property acquired through those earnings. The implementation of the commission recommendation would mitigate the financial security of full-time homemakers.

Care of Children

In fact, the commission recognised the need to offer other kinds of help to homemakers, as well as to working women. If the commission's devotion to the ideal of motherhood tempered its commitment to equality of treatment for women, its belief in free choice moderated its stand on who could care for children. The commission understood that unless women received some help in raising their children, educational and employment opportunity had little value. Moreover, as the commission repeatedly pointed out, mothers of young children did hold jobs outside the home, and these children needed supervision.

Therefore, the Commission strongly endorsed an extensive day-care programme.

The last time federal dollars had been allocated for day care was during World War II, and even then the provision of services had met less than 10 percent of the presumed need. The Children's bureau, located in the Department of Health, Education and Welfare (HEW), published a study in 1958 which asserted that four hundred thousand youngsters under the age of twelve lacked adequate arrangements for care; nevertheless, the Eisenhower administration opposed government funding of childcare centres. The National Conference on Day Care for Children, held in Washington in November 1960, recommended a comprehensive programme of day care, supported by federal and state money, and during the 1960 campaign John Kennedy had promised his support in a letter to Elinor Guggenheimer, a founder of the day-care movement in New York State. Guggenheimer, now heading a group called the National Committee on Day Care, met with the new secretaries of HEW and Labour in 1961, and won a provision for funding in the administration bill regarding amendments to the Social Security Act. Peterson strongly supported Guggenheimer's goals of day care for children of working mothers and placed her on the Home and Community Committee.

By the time the committee gathered for its first meeting in May 1962, however, Congress was close to enacting a day-care funding law that aimed not to care for the children of mothers already at work or to give those mothers who wished to work the opportunity to do so, but rather to force the mothers of young children into the labour force, a goal anathema to the Women's Bureau coalition reformers working with the president's commission. The Public Welfare Amendments, signed into law in July 1962, authorised money only for day care for children on public assistance and implied that the service was to be provided so that the mothers of children receiving public assistance could be forced to work for wages. Congress apparently believed that middle-class taxpayers wanted impoverished, unmarried, disproportionately black women to leave their children in the care of others and take paying jobs, although they disdained middle-class women who chose to do so themselves.

The commission usually deferred to prevailing political sentiments, but it could not do so in this case because insisting that lower-class mothers work contravened the philosophy of the Women's Bureau coalition, which expressly promoted the protection of women and children. Ideally, the commission believed, mothers should care for their young children at home regardless of class. The commission came out against using day-care services to support coercion of welfare recipients to work for wages and expressed sorrow for low income women who did leave babies in the care of others. The Committee on Home and Community declared that women with small children should not "be forced by economic necessity or the policies of welfare agencies" to seek outside employment, and the full commission labelled the practice "regrettable."

The commission declined to support day care as a coercive measure, but still it emphasised the need for such services. Both the committee and the commission maintained that day care should be available to families at all income levels, to provide for the children of mothers already working and to permit mothers who wanted to join the labour force to do so. They also contended that full-time homemakers who desired to devote a portion of their energy to the community or who had to meet other family needs should also have access to day-care facilities.

Although the provision of day-care services would help some women take advantage of the new opportunities the commission proposed, it could not completely resolve the dilemma of reconciling family obligations and equal chances for women in the public sphere—nor did the commission intend it to. Day care could assist women, especially those who needed to work, but the final responsibility for young children lay with the mother, and the commission presumed that she would still devote a large portion of her life to childrearing. The commission believed that women's maternal functions made them different from men in both motivation and career aspirations; therefore, it could not see forcing employers to invest equally in the training of women—equality at work would have to yield to a greater imperative of motherhood. Fatherhood implied not childcare but financial support.

In all its recommendations, the commission sought to correct the clearest injustices, to remove anachronistic obstacles to women's participation in public life, to affirm the desirability of equal treatment and the unfettered expression of individual talents, and to serve obvious and unfulfilled social needs. In doing so, however, the commission also resolved to remain firmly within the framework of traditional family roles. In making this choice, the commission reflected the ambivalence of the culture it served.

The Impact of the Presidents Commission

The President's Commission on the Status of Women took trouble to see that interest in women's status did not end with the submission of its report. In order to monitor the implementation of its proposals, and to serve as a reminder that the problems persisted, the commission asked the president in its final proposal to appoint two continuing federal bodies: an interdepartmental committee and a citizens' advisory council to "evaluate progress made, provide counsel, and serve as a means for suggesting and stimulating action". John Kennedy established the two groups on November 1, 1963; it was the next-to-last executive order he signed.

The outlook seemed hopeful. The establishment of the president's commission had raised the expectations of those concerned about women. In her bestseller, *The Feminine Mystique*, published in February 1963, Betty Friedan had written: "The very existence of the President's Commission on the Status of Women, under Eleanor Roosevelt's leadership, creates a climate where it is possible to recognise and do something about discrimination against women, in terms not only of pay but of the subtle brriers to opportunity.

Moreover, to ensure that its proposals would find a sympathetic response, the president's commission had made a sustained effort throughout its deliberations to reach out to those women's organisations that it viewed as its primary sources of support, the members of the Women's Bureau coalition. The commission had asked for the assistance of these organisations when searching for data to support its recommendations, requesting information about their experiences with protective labour legislation, their knowledge of employment and statutory discrimination, and their familiarity with court cases involving sex bias. The women's organisations reciprocated the commission's interest. Most responded to commission queries at length, many wrote articles in their newsletters, and the National Council of Catholic Women distributed sixteen thousand commission brochures. Only one organisation had a less than satisfactory relationship with the commission. The National Women's party, although it participated in every commission-related function to which it was invited, viewed the commission with justified suspicion about the Equal Rights Amendment; and for her part, Esther Peterson, who invited the NWP to all appropriate commission functions, regarded the organisation as intractable.

The recalcitrance of the NWP notwithstanding, the enthusiasm of the women's associations even outside the traditional Women's Bureau coalition had resulted in the development of an entirely new set of institutions at the state level concerned with the status of women. In November 1962, the National Federation of Business and Professional Women's Clubs notified Peterson that it wanted to undertake a programme to encourage every governor to appoint a state commission patterned after the "excellent structure" of the president's commission. The leaders of the organisation asked for a meeting with the president to get his approval of their plan, and, at Peterson's request, he complied, endorsing the proposal. The governor of the state of Washington was the first to respond to the federation's campaign; he appointed a commission in February 1963 based closely on the president's model. At the same time, he issued an executive order asking for a review of state employment regulations to ensure that they did not discriminate against women. The states of Indiana and Illinois quickly followed, as did many others, often with the assistance of the regional offices of the Women's Bureau. Although some other women's organisations resented the primary role of the BPW, during the presidential commission's lifetime ten state commissions on women were formed, and by 1967 every state had created one. The state commission movement indicated widespread national support for the president's commission; moreover, because the state commissions looked to it for their lead, they gave the parent body increased visibility and influence.

In addition to inspiring state commissions, holding meetings with women's organisations, and inviting the participation of almost two hundred citizens on its committees, the commission had enlarged its base of support through "consultations" with special interest groups. Altogether, the commission held four such consultations; three of them, "Women in the Mass Media," "Private Employment," and "New Patterns in Volunteer Work," brought in delegates from relevant organisations in an effort to explore issues and win potential allies.

Only in the fourth consultation, on the problems of Negro women, did the commission address the black women specifically, even though it generally acknowledged in its discussions that virtually every disability affected black women more severely than white. In preparation for the consultation, the staff furnished a paper that described how pending recommendations of the president's commission, such as the extension of minimum wage laws, would assist minority women. Danier Patrick Moynihan, special assistant to the secretary of labour, believed that the staff paper gave insufficient attention to the fact that "Negro society in America," according to his "limited understanding," was still "substantially a matriarchy," and did not address methods by which male-headed families could be established "if that is what is needed." The people attending the consultation—educators, editors of black magazines, representatives of the New York Urban League, and government officials—agreed with Moynihan that the black family was matriarchal, a situation forced on them, they said, by lack of job opportunities for black males. They therefore advocated better, black-run community programmes and the inclusion of Afro-American history and culture in the elementary school curriculum to provide male models for black children. The participants also raised an objection to the idea of forcing mothers of AFDC (Aid to Families with Dependent Children) families to work. In general, the consultation revealed that black women considered racial bias, not sex discrimination, their major handicap. For the commission, the consultation provided evidence of its concern for the opinions of black leaders as well as white. But whereas the commission recognised the special hardships of black women, it rejected an analogy between discrimination based on sex and discrimination based on race, and between remedies for racism and those for sex bias.

The commission formally ended its work with the presentation of its report to the president on October 11, 1963, Eleanor Roosevelt's birthday. Press coverage of the report was widespread. The *New York Times* gave it front-page space, the Associated Press devoted a four-part series to it, and the "Today" show on NBC television offered a live interview with Peterson on the day of the presentation. More than one newspaper editorial observed that the commission was inconsistent in maintaining that a woman's first responsibility was to her family in the home and then expecting employers to treat her the same way they did male employees; the *Wall Street Journal* found the commission's proposal for day care "a tinge . . . collectivist." On the whole, however, these views were exceptional. Most women's magazines and journals of women's organisations, after summarising the report's contents, commended it to their readers.

White House advisers concluded that, with the presentation of the commission report, the Kennedy administration had put together a worthy record on behalf of women, regardless of the number of women appointees. In preparation for the presentation ceremony, Myer Feldman recounted for the president the list of achievements. Most had proceeded from the agenda laid out in the Women's Bureau: the presidential commission's study; equal pay legislation; the ruling against discrimination in the civil service; the elimination of a quota system for women officers in the armed forces (undertaken also at the request of the president's commission); and the extension of the Fair Labour Standards Act to include retail workers, many of whom were women. Feldman also included the establishment of a consumer advisory council, which Kennedy had pledged in his campaign, and the provision of money for day care. The administration was justified in regarding the President's Commission on the Status of Women as the jewel in its crown for women.

Constrained by its refusal to examine the conflicts in defining roles by sex, its search for unanimity, and its desire for political acceptability, the PCSW often left the hardest problems untackled and forswore the most potent solutions; nevertheless, taken all together, the recommendations of the president's commission broke new ground. Were it brought to fruition, the agenda formulated by the commission would improve opportunities for women outside the home and enhance support within it. For the first time, a federal body examined the status of women, found it wanting, and offered prescriptions for its improvement. It decreed the problem of sex discrimination legitimate, insisting that it hurt not only the individual but also the nation. In doing so, the commission responded to a social reality and a social need. Although not far ahead of public opinion, the president's commission, by openly acknowledging the validity of the quest for equal treatment, nudged public opinion along.

Commission proposals covered the range of problems observed by each of the three interest groups of women in the fifteen years since World War II and forged them into a unified agenda. Like the Women's Bureau coalition, the President's Commission on the Status of Women suggested many "specific bills for specific ills." The committee asked the federal government to assume responsibility for encouraging private employers to treat women workers equitably and requested both public and private enterprises to provide women with the chance to work part-time so that they could acquire or use their skills while at the same time meeting their family responsibilities. Both federal and state legislation, counselled the commission, should mandate minimum wages for men and women, premium pay for overtime, and equal wages for men and women performing equal work. The commission maintained that unemployment insurance coverage had to offer women better protection and that employers, trade unions, and government at all levels should unite to develop a programme of maternity benefits that would remove some of the burden from women who bore all the costs of having and rearing children. The commission advocated that the federal government permit more generous tax deductions for childcare and that local, state, and federal governments finance both educational programmes and skilled counselling assistance sensitive to needs of women at all stages of their lives. The commission proposed community childcare facilities, with costs shared publicly and privately, so that women might take advantage of better educational opportunities and employment possibilities. Like ERA advocates, the commission endorsed the need for an affirmation of constitutional equality for women, as well as a movement to expunge from state legal codes antiquated laws that discriminated against women, barring them, for example, from jury service or hampering their right to own or convey property or change their domicile. Following the counsel of political party women, and to ensure that the legal system would become more responsive to women's needs, the commission encouraged women, political parties, and appointing officials to see that more women participated on government. The president's commission combined and endorsed all the separate agendas, permitting the boundaries that had separated the groups before to fade into the background.

Three weeks after the submission of the report, Kennedy completed his actions on behalf of American women by creating the continuing groups the commission had recommended, the Interdepartmental Committee and the Citizens Advisory Council on the Status of Women. In the executive order, the president declared: "Enhancement of the quality of American life, as envisioned by the Commission's report, can be accomplished only through concerted action by both public and private groups, through coordinated action within the Federal Government, and through action by States, communities, educational institutions, voluntary organisations, employers, unions, and individual citizens." Further federal initiatives would take place under a new administration.

In her memorandum to Secretary of Labour Arthur Goldberg proposing the establishment of a commission on women, Esther Peterson had argued that the commission would not only block the Equal Rights Amendment, but it also would "help the nation . . . move further towards full partnership, creative use of skills, and genuine equality of opportunity." As Peterson intended, the President's Commission on the Status of Women had important implications for the politics of women's issues in the 1960s. It drew opposing interest groups together, narrowing the gap between the Women's Bureau coalition and ERA advocates; it enunciated a federal policy against sex discrimination, affirming that women, like men, had a right to paid employment; it presented a cogent set of proposals to begin the amelioration of the difficulties women faced; it built up networks of support among women's organisations and served as the model for analogous institutions on the state level; and, at its conclusion, it provided for a continuing presence at the federal level, to ensure that the consideration of the status of women would not disappear with the termination of the commission. But only indirectly did the commission foster its most important sequel; a resurgent, energetic, widespread women's movement that arose from the active politics of the 1960s.

7

A Model for Action for Women's Rights

After the conclusion of the President's Commission on the Status of Women, female activists within the federal government and the state commissions strove to improve opportunities for women, using the commission's agenda as a guide. The transfer of power from John Kennedy to Lyndon Johnson, who was strongly sensitive to the exigencies of political patronage, engendered new attention for appointments of women; yet Johnson strongly supported the plan of the president's commission, going so far as to mute his own endorsement of the Equal Rights Amendment. As the attempt to find a case suitable for Supreme Court adjudication languished, the success of a new civil rights bill soon presented ERA proponents with an unexpected opportunity to take a swipe at the recommendations; the result of their action was to give women new and unprecedented protection against employment discrimination. Official resistance to the new law, however, bred resentment among women nationwide—and as the number of women aware of women's equity issues grew, so did the seeds of a grassroots movement.

Lyndon Johnson

Following John Kennedy's assassination, Lyndon Johnson came into office with several goals. Painfully aware of Kennedy's popularity, Johnson sought to prove himself faithful to the objectives of his predecessor and win equal affection. A southerner, but now distances from his Texas constituency, Johnson wanted to display his commitment to equalising treatment for blacks, to eliminating poverty in America, and to bringing the war in Vietnam to a successful conclusion. In pursuit of these ends, Johnson presided over liberalism's "greatest triumphs and sharpest defeats," as historian William Chafe characterised the events of Johnson's tenure. Under the new president's guidance, Congress enacted path-breaking civil rights laws and produced legislation providing federal aid to education, housing, medicare, mental health programmes, urban mass transit, preschool for underprivileged children, employment and training programmes, environmental and consumer programmes. Johnson's "War on Poverty" lifted the incomes of millions of American families.

Kennedy's assassination and the murders of black leaders Medgar Evers in 1963 and Malcolm X in 1965, together with Johnson's encouragement of civil rights legislation and his pursuit of the Vietnam War, all fuelled the social protest in the 1960s. In 1962, a nascent student movement emerged seeking to quell militarism and to join with the civil rights movement in the cause of racial equality; by 1968, Students for a Democratic Society counted one hundred thousand members. Peaceful demonstration proved an inadequate force for halting the war, however, and campuses exploded in protest in 1968. Meanwhile, urban ghettos were beset by waves of violence, and in the spring of 1968 civil rights leader Martin Luther King, Jr., and Robert F. Kennedy, who was running in the Democratic primaries as a peace candidate, were both murdered.

Although the national community seemed truly to be coming apart, by the mid-1970s the eruptions of angry protest had abated. The antiwar movement was defused by troop reductions and the elimination of the draft. Black leaders turned from street demonstrations to more traditional politics. Yet out of the turmoil of the 1960s, from both the government's commitment to moderate, controlled social change and the New Left's objective of radical social reorganisation, was born a vital women's movement that endured for another decade.

"Crypto-Feminism"

The policy initiatives of the Kennedy years had taken place against a backdrop of widening activity by women, continuing the trend that had intensified after World War II. Between 1960 and 1965 the number of bachelor's and first professional degrees earned by women increased 57 percent, compared with only a 25 percent increase for men. By 1968 women were earning about one-third of all master's degrees and 13 percent of doctorates. The more educated the woman, the more likely she was to work outside the home, and by 1968 women represented 37 percent of the labour force, up 3 percent since 1960. The increase for married women was even more significant: in 1960, 30.6 percent of married women worked: by 1968, that figure had grown to 37 percent.

What these figures did not reveal, however, was that, relative to white men, white women had declined in economic position throughout the postwar period. Of full-time workers in 1966, women earned only 58.2 percent of the income of men, down from 63.3 percent in 1956. Women with college degrees, a growing proportion of women workers, were still earning less than men with only high school educations. As more and more college-educated women entered the labour market, they encountered opportunities far narrower than their male peers enjoyed.

Working women did not suffer only economic disadvantages; they also paid an emotional price for joining the workforce. Throughout the fifteen-year postwar period, publications both popular and scholarly suggested that American women who assumed nonconventional roles were neglecting their families or losing their femininity. The country continued to prefer that women not openly challenge men professionally or intellectually. By the early 1960s, journalists were describing a "prevailing malaise" among women as a result of the conflict between women's achievements and traditional norms. Marya Mannes protests in the *New York Times Magazine* that intellectual women were victimised because American men were uncomfortable with them, and an essay in the *Commonweal* lamented that an honest, intelligent woman had inevitably to become a social rebel because American society did not really approve of forceful, thinking women. In October 1962, the editors of *Harper's* published a special supplement in recognition of the "important changes" that had taken place in the roles of women. In this issue, such authors as psychologist Bruno Bettelheim argued that women who had been educated like men experienced frustration when confronted after graduation by limitations for intellectual expression. *Harper's* called the nascent disquiet "crypto-feminism."

The discussion in the popular press of the plight of the American woman culminated in February 1963 in the publication of *The feminine Mystique* by Betty Friedan. In evaluating information garnered from a questionnaire sent in 1957 to her 1942 classmates at Smith College, Friedan had detected a "problem that has no name," which displayed itself in the breakdown of the mental and physical health of college-educated homemakers who were living through their husbands and children. Friedan argued that women needed creative work of their own and that women's life plans had to integrate marriage and motherhood with independent work in order for them to be healthy individuals.

The "problem that has no name," "malaise", and "crypto-feminism" all referred to the strain between customary expectations for women and the changing circumstances of American life. Greater numbers of highly educated women, believing it to be best for their families if they did not work for pay, found themselves stultified by the lack of intellectually stimulating outlets while they were home. Then they faced three potentially useful decades after their children had grown, but often lacked skills and experience to permit an easy transition to the workplace. Those women with children who were forced to work by the exigencies of a consumer society discovered severely circumscribed possibilities for employment and advancement and in addition suffered criticism for leaving their families ostensibly without proper care.

Yet women did not, in the early 1960s, organise themselves to alleviate such difficulties. As Jo Freeman has pointed out, "Social strain does not create social movements; it only creates the potential for movements." The "social strain" described had in fact characterised the entire postwar period, leading finally to the call for a national commission on women. That commission's report, *American Women,* now served as a focus of discussion for the state commissions set up to emulate the national group, a nationwide system of commissions on women that, as Freeman described it, created a "climate of expectations" for potential action.

American Women followed the appearance of Friedan's book by only six months, and the reaction to it, in both demand for copies and continuing formation of state commissions, indicated that the chord struck by these publications had wide reverberations. By October 1964 the government had distributed eighty-three thousand copies of *American Women* (which had also been translated into three languages: Japanese, Swedish, and Italian), and in 1965 Charles Scribner's Sons published a commercial version edited by Margaret Mead.

The Citizens' Advisory Council and the Interdepartmental Committee on the Status of Women

President Johnson was eager to capitalise on the good will engendered by the commission. As vice-president, Johnson had made known his strong support of the commission's objectives and had often attended commission functions; following the group's first meeting it was Mrs. Johnson, not Jacqueline Kennedy, who hosted the reception for the assembled representatives. Shortly after Johnson took over, Elizabeth Carpenter, Mrs. Johnson's press secretary, called Esther Peterson to ask her advice on how to win for the new president the support of the women's organisations that had so enthusiastically backed the president's commission. Peterson replied that Johnson should appoint commission member Margaret Hickey to chair the Citizens' Advisory Council on the Status of Women (CACSW)—a decision John Kennedy already made but not implemented—and that this appointment would signal his intention to stand behind the commission's work. Johnson dutifully followed the advice, and both he and Mrs. Johnson attended the council's first meeting. In Women's Bureau releases, Esther Peterson moved quickly to identify Johnson with the Kennedy policy initiatives on women.

The Interdepartmental Committee on the Status of Women (ICSW) and the CACSW were continuations of the president's commission not only in spirit but also in personnel. The executive order establishing the ICSW and the CACSW placed in the former group all the cabinet members who had been on the president's commission, plus the secretaries of state and defense. John Kennedy named to the CACSW all the nongovernment members of the presidential commission, adding Eleanor Roosevelt's daughter, Anna Halsted, and the president of the Trenton Trust Company, Mary Roebling. The support of the two continuing groups, with membership almost identical to that of the president's commission, signified that there would be no sharp departure in the Johnson administration from the agenda described in the commission report.

The new president chose, however, to highlight one particular recommendation in order to differentiate himself from his predecessor and to win some new and exciting publicity before the 1964 election. His decision provided a momentary return to the modus operandi of Kennedy's predecessors. In January 1964, Lyndon Johnson declared to a *Washington Post* reporter that he intended to appoint fifty women to significant policy-making positions within thirty days; the story appeared on the front page. Johnson, a longtime party man, endorsed the notion that the appointments were good politics, and he responded to the suggestions of party women with whom he had long been associated—and whose counsel, to their delight and relief, was once again welcome in the White House. The president's closest female adviser, Elizabeth Carpenter, originally a journalist, saw good public relations in the campaign to appoint women and encouraged the president to do so.

Indeed, Johnson's actions led to a sharp increase in the number of women serving in Senate-confirmed positions, with ten such appointments in his first thirteen months in office—excluding local customs office jobs, the same number as Kennedy had named during his whole three years. Of these ten, six represented "firsts" for women, compared to four for Kennedy. During the balance of his term, Johnson appointed another seventeen women. Of the twenty-seven total appointments, sixteen were firsts, and the number of women serving in the administration rose from thirty in 1963 to fifty-two in 1968. Although Johnson did not name a woman to his cabinet, he was not criticised for this omission—an indication that his overall record, with due attention given to breaking new ground, contented Democratic women. Moreover, thanks to Liz Carpenter, Johnson accompanied his appointments with the fanfare political women thought appropriate. Yet unlike Truman and Eisenhower, Johnson also took an interest in the civil service efforts the presidential commission had instigated. Rapid gains in high-level jobs for women took place at the beginning of 1964. Party women were very pleased, and the journalist Isabelle Shelton recalled more than a decade later: "There's never been anything like it—before or since."

But Johnson's burst of interest in appointments created some unforeseen consequences that affected the status of women more significantly than the mere numbers of nominees. By pledging a larger role for women in his administration, Johnson raised expectations that he then failed to fulfil. The appointments campaign ended with the 1964 presidential election, and by March 1965 Margaret Price complained once again that women were dissatisfied with the number of staff appointments. This time the displeasure spread through the state commissions, gaining attention from many more women—women organised and focused on the status of women—than ever before.

A second outcome of Johnson's appointments concerned the Women's Bureau. The president designated Esther Peterson to be his special assistant on consumer affairs, the single highest post to which he named a woman. (India Edwards and Liz Carpenter both observed the irony in giving this post to Peterson, who already was the ranking female member of the administration as assistant secretary of labour, a job she retained. Both women pointed out that Johnson would be able to name more women to important jobs if Peterson did not get them all. In fact, Peterson became one of the few Kennedy appointees Johnson continued to trust.) With the new appointment, Peterson decided to relinquish the directorship of the Women's Bureau, the least prestigious of the three jobs she held, and Johnson replaced her with Mary Dublin Keyserung, an economist active in Democratic politics.

Keyserling was not pleased by the new position of conciliation the president's commission had crafted. A longtime worker with the national Consumers League, Keyserling maintained a firm commitment to its philosophy that working women required protection, a point of view she had expressed emphatically while serving on the Committee on Protective Labour Legislation of the commission. Secretary of Labour Willard Wirtz shared Keyserling's view, as expressed in the president's commission report, that hours laws for women should be expanded until they could be replaced by laws requiring premium pay for overtime. As Peterson and Catherine East, formerly the technical secretary of the Committee on Federal employment and now the executive secretary of the Citizens' Advisory Council on the Status of Women, moved away from the idea of maintaining laws that protected women and not men, they came into increasing conflict with Keyserling and Wirtz.

Title VII

The issue became of great moment with the consideration of the 1964 omnibus civil rights bill. Introduced by Representative Emanuel Celler (D-N.Y.) in June 1963, the comprehensive civil rights bill strengthened voting rights and access to public education for black Americans and prohibited discrimination based or race in places of public accommodation in federally assisted programmes, and in employment. The House Judiciary Committee held hearings on the bill for twenty-two days, reporting it favourably on November 20, 1963, two days before President Kennedy was assassinated. Sex discrimination had not been mentioned.

The National Woman's party reacted to the committee report with a resolution, passed in December, that bemoaned the fact that the bill "would not even give protection against discrimination because of 'race, colour, religion, or national origin,' to a *White Woman*, a *Woman of the Christian Religion* or a *Woman of United States Origin*." With this statement, the NWP began its campaign to amend the bill to include a prohibition against sex discrimination.

Although the party maintained that the ERA constituted all the protection women needed, given that such an amendment did not exist, party members had always sought to have women included in fair employment practices legislation and executive orders applying to minorities. The NWP did not initiate such legislation, because its largely privileged and conservative membership generally believed that the government should not intervene in private enterprise. However, if the federal government insisted on offering protection to black workers, the NWP did not want women placed at a relative disadvantage by being denied similar assistance.

The party quickly turned to a powerful ally, Representative

Howard Smith (D-Va.), the chairman of the House Rules Committee and a longtime proponent of the Equal Rights Amendment. An archconservative Southerner, Smith, in common with many NWP members, opposed the whole idea of the bill. If the addition of *sex* to Title VII, the employment title of the pending civil rights statute, were to result in the bill's demise, Smith, and several NWP members, would be satisfied. Yet if the bill were to pass, Smith agreed with the NWP that it had to include women in its scope: otherwise white women would lack an advantage granted to black men. In addition to seeking Smith's backing, the NWP also approached women members of Congress. The party met resistance, however, Wither because the women representatives perceived a lack of support from other members or because they had promised the administration not to offer amendments on the floor. Finally Representatives Martha Griffiths (D-Mich.) and Katharine St. George (R-N.Y.), both strong supporters of the ERA, decided to back the amendment but to let Howard Smith introduce it, pointing out that his endorsement would bring many votes they themselves could not acquire. During the hearings on the rule, Smith quizzed Celler about the omission of sex as a prohibited basis for discrimination and warned that he intended to offer an amendment to eliminate the gap. On January 26, White House correspondent May Craig raised the issue with Smith on the television show "Meet the Press", and Smith agreed again to consider it.

The Women's Bureau coalition opposed adding sex as a prohibited basis of discrimination on two grounds. For one thing, the President's Commission on the Status of Women had asserted that race and sex discrimination were best treated separately, and the coalition continued to endorse this view. Banning sex discrimination in the same way as racial bias threatened protective labour laws. Then, like most liberal reformers, the members of the coalition believed that the fight against racism had prior claim. The year 1964 was, once again, the "Negro's hour," and many liberal women believed that the issue of women's rights had been raised merely to kill the bill with another controversial clause. As before, the two factions were at loggerheads.

On February 8, 1964, as he had suggested he would, Howard Smith introduced an amendment to add the word *sex* to Title VII of the pending civil rights bill. Assuring the House that he was "very serious" about the proposal, Smith insisted that it could not do the measure any harm and that it might in fact improve it. After he discussed the issue of discrimination against women in employment, however, Smith read excerpts, with an excess of chivalry, from a letter he had received complaining that some women were cheated out of husbands because there were too few men to go around. He warned his colleagues to take note of such "real grievances." Celler responded with similar jocularity, pointing out that he usually had the last two words in his household of women, and they were "Yes, dear." Other members found the exchange highly amusing. Celler then offered serious objections to the amendment, citing first a Department of Labour letter quoting Esther Peterson, who reiterated the position of the president's commission that sex discrimination was best treated separately and who argued that the addition of sex to Title VII would "not be to the best advantage of women at this time." Celler contended that the provision would reproduce the language of the pending Equal Rights Amendment, and he opposed it on that basis, referring to alimony, compulsory military service for women, custody, and rape laws—none of them relevant to the proposal at hand, which dealt only with employment. The germane point he raised concerned protective labour laws: Celler warned that enacting the proposal under discussion might result in the nullification of state legislation regulating hours and conditions of women's work.

After Celler and Smith finished, all but one of the twelve women members of the House rose ("suddenly", according to the *New York Times*) to speak in favour of the amendment. Martha Griffiths, prepared for the occasion, pointed out that the laughter surrounding the introduction of the amendment exposed the second-class citizenship of American women. Her concern, she said, was that the bill as written would leave white women with no protection at all, because black women would have a cause of action against employers who hired only white men, but white women would not. She dismissed the argument concerning labour legislation: the main function of such laws, she said, had been to protect men's rights to better-paying jobs. But she suggested that a clause to save protective laws would be feasible if that were the price of labour support. Griffiths concluded by declaring that a vote against the amendment by a white man was a vote against his wife, his widow, his daughter, and his sister.

The one woman legislator who spoke against the amendment was Edith Green, former member of the president's commission, who risked, she said, being deemed an "Aunt Jane." Nevertheless, she argued, discrimination against blacks was more severe than against women, and she could not support and amendment that would jeopardize the bill as a whole. Green further noted that not one organisation had submitted testimony in favour of this change to the committees considering it. Later in the debate she voiced the argument that biological differences between men and women would spell trouble for employers forced to hire women. Despite Green's protest, however, after a two-hour discussion the coalition of women legislators in favour of equality for women, Republicans in sympathy with the ERA, and opponents of civil rights legislation seeking to block passage of the bill added sex discrimination to the ban in the pending legislation by a vote of 168 to 133. Two days later the House passed the entire bill 290 to 130. All the men but one who had spoken in favour of the sex amendment voted against the bill.

Predictably, response to the sex provision was mixed. The National Woman's party rejoiced, as did the congresswomen who had supported the proposal. The Women's Division of the United Automobile Workers, which had always favoured compulsory measures to eliminate sex discrimination, also applauded. Esther Peterson, however, expressed fear that the amendment might hurt the bill's chances in the Senate and insisted that, in any case, discrimination based on sex warranted separate treatment. A *Washington Post* editorial facetiously concluded that the vote made it "pretty plain . . . who's head of the House up there on the Hill."

The newly formed Citizens' Advisory Council on the Status of Women held its first meeting two days after the House vote and, at the request of the Justice Department, made no statement. The CACSW had a commitment to implement the presidential commission's recommendations opposing such a law, but Assistant Attorney General Burke Marshall told the council that the bill's passage represented the "most important thing" and that employment opportunity for women was "a side matter", regardless of commission proposals. According to Marshall, the administration was indifferent as to whether the bill passed with the sex amendment or without it; its only concern was to decide in which form the bill's chances were best. Dorothy Height, the president of the National Council of Negro Women, spoke of a two-part dilemma: she feared on the one hand that the inclusion of sex would weaken the administration of the bill with respect to race, which clearly came first for her; but on the other she also feared that any discussion about the ill effects of the sex amendment might weaken the support for the bill as a whole, by providing an excuse for someone to vote against it. Marshall agreed, and asked the CACSW to take no position. The council readily assented, without even discussing the bill's implications for women. Because it would not meet again until the fall, the council thus played no role in the enactment of legislation prohibiting sex discrimination in employment.

Eager to avoid a conference on the bill, the White House decided to seek a Senate vote on the measure exactly as it had passed the House, including the sex proviso. The women in the House of Representatives lobbied among the senators for the amendment, and Pauli Murray, as a black woman sensitive to the problems of both racial and sex-based discrimination and they dynamic between them, circulated a memorandum that maintained that the omission of *sex* would weaken the civil rights bill by once again dividing the interests of oppressed groups in the society and by neglecting the problems of black women. In support of her argument, Murray, then on the faculty of Yale Law School, quoted at length from the documents of the president's commission. Ironically, then, the discussion by the commission, which had not recommended fair employment legislation for women, of the problem of discrimination against women, together with its inclusion of dissenting opinions in its publications, furthered the cause of the new bill.

The National Woman's party continued to play a major role in the controversy, forming a special emergency committee to watch over the sex provision. When Senator Everett Dirksen spoke against it, the NWP asked ERA supporter Margaret Chase Smith, the only female Republican senator, to intervene. The Illinois BPW organised an intensive lobbying campaign directed at Dirksen, who finally acquiesced. Although the attempt to have the Senate pass the House measure without any amendment did not succeed, on June 17 the Senate did endorse a substitute bill, with the sex discrimination clause included, by a vote of seventy-six to eighteen. Two weeks later, on July 2, 1964, the House adopted the Senate bill with more than two thirds voting in favour. Lyndon Johnson signed the measure into law the same day.

Thus, by 1964 a situation unique in the postwar period prevailed: in the absence of a widespread women's movement, a federal law had been passed that prohibited sex discrimination in employment, thanks to EPA advocates who took advantage of both the administration's eagnerness to protect the welfare of black citizens and the desire of Southern legislators to thwart that effort. Two federal advisory groups and a national network of commissions on women, all the work of the Women's Bureau coalition, existed for the purpose of examining the status of women in the context of a stated federal policy of equality rendered first by the president's commission and now by Congress as well.

This combination of partial successes on the part of both the Women's Bureau coalition and the proponents of the ERA in the early sixties led to raised expectations and tools with which to organise. An atmosphere now obtained in which the discontent, born of the disjuncture among the ideals of womanhood, the changing conditions of women's lives, and the unrealised promise of equality, could find constructive expression. The unforeseen backlash that greeted the new sex discrimination law proved to be the catalyst for action.

Acting on the PSCW Agenda

The President's Commission on the Status of Women had not predicted or advocated so sweeping a legal measure of Title VII of the 1964 Civil Rights Act, and at the beginning its heirs preferred to ignore it and concentrate on their more moderate agenda. As a result of PSCW recommendations, civil service health benefits were equalised, the Departments of State and Defense revised regulations on dependency allowances, and the Department of Labour amended rules for eligibility of federal apprenticeship programmes to prohibit sex bias. Congress also raised the income level for tax deductions for childcare. In 1966 the Department of Health Education, and Welfare inaugurated a policy of supplying birth control information and devices on request. Federal funds supported pilot programmes in the counselling of girls and mature women. Amendments to the Fair Labour Standards Act left only 5.4 million women and 6 million men uncovered. As of November 1966, more than $3 million had been found owing in equal pay violations and the secretary of labour had brought thirty cases to court.

Also in keeping with the position of the PCSW, the Johnson administration did not support the ERA, even though Lyndon Johnson had as a senator endorsed the amendment. National Woman's party members had believed that his accession to the presidency presaged a favourable change in White House policy, but Johnson could not take over for Kennedy and immediately disown the presidential commission's recommendation on so crucial a matter. He publicly backed the Fourteenth Amendment strategy the commission had ultimately proposed. In December 1963, Peterson drafted a position statement for White House letters that announced: "The President is impressed by the Commission's position and believes that this approach should be fully explored before considering a new constitutional amendment on this subject." To the dissatisfaction of ERA proponents, the White House followed her line. Amendment adherents were further distressed when Johnson saw to it that the 1964 Democratic Party platform contained no reference to the ERA. Emma Guffey Miller wrote bitterly to Johnson, whom she admired intensely:

> As one who has grown old in the service of the Democratic Party may I tell you . . . of the deep disappointment of many thousands of Democratic women like myself who question the right of Mrs. Esther Peterson to assume the leadership of the Democratic women and dictate the womans [sic] plank in our 1964 platform. . . . Now [it] omits the Equal Rights plank for women, a plank which has been adopted by our party for two decades. This is not progress, Mr. President, but retrogression.

Other support for the amendment rapidly declined After 1964 the Senate Judiciary Committee ceased reporting the amendment out, and in 1968 the Republicans dropped the amendment from their platform as well. Many members of Congress responded to letters on the ERA by informing constituents of the PSCW plan for constitutional equality.

In 1965 a case finally appeared that looked as though it might yield the Supreme Court interpretation the commission had sought and result in unity with ERA adherents. The hope proved short-lived. Black residents, both men and women, of Lowndes County, Alabama, represented by the American Civil Liberties Union (ACLU), filed a suit in federal district court charging that methods of jury selection of Lowndes County contravened the Fourteenth Amendment in excluding blacks by practice and women by state law. Mary Eastwood, Pauli Murray, Marguerite Rawalt, and Catherine East, all connected by their association on the president's commission, worked to gather to obtain amicus briefs from various women's organisations, and the Justice Department intervened at Esther Peterson's request. Pauli Murray helped draft the ACLU brief, looking forward to Supreme Court review. When the federal district court ruled in favour of the plaintiffs, however, the state of Alabama did not appeal. Although the Citizens' Advisory Council on the Status of Women declared the district court decision a "landmark victory for women's rights," the absence of a Supreme Court ruling made the event inconclusive. Proponents of the PCSW position continued to seek a Supreme Court declaration, but to no avail.

At the same time, because of the President's Commission on the Status of Women, hundreds of women and men were involved in state commissions actively fighting on local fronts for women's rights. The CACSW devoted the major part of its attention to monitoring programmes of women's organisations and state commissions in fulfilment of the presidential commission's agenda for women. Their activity brought results and, concomitantly, an expectation of further change. In the two and a half years after the commission's report, six states enacted minimum wage laws that applied to both men and women, and nine more states extended previously existing minimum wage laws for women to cover men as well. Eleven states took action to make hours laws for women more flexible, three repealed such laws, and six adopted laws providing for overtime pay for work in excess of a certain number of hours. Nine states enacted equal pay laws, bringing to thirty-five the number of states with some equal pay protection. Spurred by local groups and federal grants, homemaker services in local communities burgeoned. Many states took action to amend various laws that restrained the rights of women to operate as freely as men. Four states modified discriminatory jury service laws, three amended statutes limiting a married women's right to dispose of her property, and several states strengthened child support laws or changed laws that prescribed one legal marriage age for men and another for women. Every year state commissions and women's organisations held conferences, published literature, created pilot programmes in cooperation with state and local governments, conducted studies, lobbied or state and federal legislation, trained volunteers, operated day-care centres and homemaker programmes, ran courses, and developed audiovisual materials for use by educators—all in the attempt to further the goals established by the president's commission. Not since World War II had women's issues received so much attention.

The scions of the PCSW brought all these activists together. In 1964, in order to establish ties among the state groups, the CACSW and the Interdepartmental Committee on the Status of Women began inviting representatives of state commissions annually to Washington for national conferences and publishing written reports of the proceedings. At the first such meeting, eighty-three representatives of commissions in thirty-one states discussed issues of equal pay, minimum wage laws, day-care facilities, equality in public employment, educational and counselling programmes for women, and derisive media treatment. By 1965 the conference had grown to more than four hundred participants from forty-four states, with eleven workshops addressing legal status, Title VII, vocational guidance, educational and employment, labour standards, income maintenance, and women in public life, as well as the financing and management of state commissions. Administration support for their efforts showed in the attendance of the president, cabinet members, and other federal officials. By now, the participants in the state commissions had combined into a national watchdog agency on women's rights; they proceeded to turn their attention to the implementation of Title VII.

The ICSW and the CACSW intended to have the state commissions follow their lead on Title VII and protective labour legislation—but their own position was not entirely clear. A subcommittee of the ICSW, composed of Evelyn Harrison, deputy for Civil Service Commission chair John Macy, Mary Eastwood, from the Justice Department, and Mary Keyserling, acting as the deputy of Secretary of Labour Willard Wirtz, set to work formulating a position. The subcommittee could not, however, reach a consensus on how the newly formed Equal Employment Opportunity Commission (EEOC) should construe the effect of Title VII on state laws. Eastwood, who had been the technical secretary of the PCSW Committee on Civil and Political Rights and who had written the attorney general's opinion in 1962 permitting John Kennedy to ban sex discrimination in the civil service, had become convinced that protective labour laws hampered women's opportunities, and she observed that more and more state commissions had arrived at the same conclusion. The Civil Service Commission had itself ruled that women federal workers were sufficiently protected by regulations to be exempted from coverage by state laws pertaining to women's employment. Harrison and Eastwood recommended that in the case of a conflict between state laws and Title VII, the state laws should be ruled inoperative. Mary Keyserling, however, continued to be committed to the traditional posture that women needed special treatment. She contended simply that no conflict existed between Title VII and state labour laws for women. The subcommittee therefore drew up two position papers for ICSW chairman Secretary of Labour Willard Wirtz to consider.

For her part, Assistant Secretary of Labour Esther Peterson was ready to concede that protective labour laws had had their day and that the Department of Labour should now move ahead to a single standard, a standard show had been ready to adopt even for the president's commission. Peterson suggested that most problems could be solved by extending protective laws to men or, where the work was of an especially heavy nature, by permitting exceptions under the "bona fide occupational qualification" provision. While Peterson admitted that the prohibition of sex discrimination in employment came before she and many others anticipated it would, it represented, to her, a "great opportunity." She proposed that the EEOC adopt the principle of a single standard and consider each law on a case-by-case basis.

Peterson, however, had moved beyond her former constituency of labour unions and traditional women's organisations, and the Department of Labour did not follow her recommendation. Rather, the consensus of the Women's Bureau coalition favoured retention of the laws. Yielding to the advice of Mary Keyserling and many labour union representatives, Willard Wirtz wrote to EEOC chairman Franklin D. Roosevelt, Jr., that Title VII did not require "a general invalidation" of protective laws, many of which, he counselled, were useful and reconcilable with the objectives of Title VII. "In general", he advised Roosevelt, "the Department believes that the Commission should follow a policy of protecting and preserving these laws wherever possible and practicable." Women's organisations, labour unions, religions groups, and civil liberties organisations, including the AFLCIO, expressed similar views to the EEOC. The CACSW, unable to reach a firm consensus among its members, merely issued a statement upholding the president's commission position on protective laws, while glossing over the key issue of Title VII's impact.

The EEOC willingly followed the advice of the Women's Bureau coalition and the Department of Labour. At the 1965 meeting of state commissions on women, hosted in July by the ICSW and the CACSW, Roosevelt assured the participants that the commission would more "with great care" regarding protective labour laws. The commission did not, Roosevelt explained, see "any clear Congressional intent to overturn all of these laws".

The Equal Employment Opportunity Commission

The EEOC's willingness to retain protective labour laws did not stem only from its concern for the opinions of the groups lobbying it; EEOC commissioners and staff also expressed a general belief that the addition of *sex* to the law had been illegitimate—merely a ploy to kill the bill—and that it did not therefore constitute a mandate to equalise women's employment opportunities. Aileen Hernandez, the only woman on the commission, later recalled that the subject of sex discrimination elicited either "boredom" or "virulent hostility." In September 1965, EEOC executive director N. Thompson Powers told Secretary Wirtz that "the Commission is very much aware of the importance of not becoming known as the 'sex commission' ". By November 1965 Herman Edelsberg had succeeded Powers, and he told the press: "There are people on this commission who think that no man should be required to have a male secretary—and I am one of them."

The commission's attitude revealed itself in both its actions and its words. Title VII included a clear ban on segregated employment advertisement; the act read: "It shall be an unlawful employment practice for an employer . . . to publish or cause to be . . . published any notice or advertisement relating to employment . . . indicating any preference, limitation, specification, or discrimination, based on race, colour, religion, sex, or national origin" except in the case of a bona fide occupational qualification. The EEOC quickly ruled that newspaper advertisements for jobs segregated by race constituted a clear transgression of the act but convened an *ad hoc* committee to determine whether sex-segregated want ads similarly violated the statute, since sex would presumably be a bona fide occupational qualification more often than race.

The committee comprised fourteen members from advertising agencies, newspapers, and business firms, two from the Department of Labour, and one from the American Nurses Association. Not surprisingly, this group, with its disproportionate representation of commercial interests, resolved that want ads segregated by sex did not contravene Title VII. Moreover, Abraham Fortas, then on the Supreme Court, reportedly told Johnson that the Court would strike down a regulation banning sex-labelled want ads as a violation of the First Amendment's free press clause. The EEOC had initially split three to two for making sex-segregated want ads illegal. Commissioners Richard Graham, a white Republican from Wisconsin, Aileen Hernandez, a black woman from California, and Sam Jackson, a black Republican from Kansas, supported the ban, with commission chairman Franklin Roosevelt Jr., and vice-chairman Luther Holcomb opposed. After Holcomb passed along Fortas's opinion from Johnson, Jackson changed his vote. In August 1965, the EEOC issued its ruling that employers could advertise in sex-segregated columns. The commission required only that newspapers publish a disclaimer informing readers that the headings were not intended to be discriminatory but only reflected that fact that some jobs were of more interest to one sex than another. The EEOC ignored the recommendation of the CACSW that advertising be sex-neutral.

Although the EEOC had issued a regulation that directly contradicted the wording of Title VII, it received criticism even for the mild restraint it had imposed on the newspapers. The ostensibly liberal *New Republic* believed the commission would have done better simply to have ignored the sex provision. "Why", asked the journal, "should a mischievous joke perpetrated on the floor of the House of Representatives be treated by a responsible administrative body with this kind of seriousness?"

The *New Republic* spoke for many; the ban on sex discrimination elicited derision and ridicule. The *Wall Street Journal,* in an article published a week before the effective date of the act, asked its readers to picture, if they could, "a shapeless, knobby-kneed male 'bunny' serving drinks to a group of stunned businessmen in a Playboy Club" or a "matronly vice-president" chasing a male secretary around her desk. EEOC's own executive director, Herman Edelsberg, reportedly circulated a suggestion that the commission seal depict a brown rabbit, together with a white rabbit "couchant", with the legend "Vive la différence". A personnel officer at a large airline described his employer as "unnerved" by the ban on sex discrimination. "What are we going to do now", the personnel officer asked, "when a gal walks into our office, demands a job as an airline pilot and has the credentials to qualify?" A manager of an electronic components company that employed only women suggested sarcastically, "I suppose we'll have to advertise for people with small, nimble fingers and hire the first male midget with unusual dexterity [who] shows up."

Business attitudes placed the EEOC on the defensive. One official told the *Wall Street Journal* that the government intended to enforce the sex prohibition with great leniency "if the women's groups will let us get away with it". Nevertheless, commission staff explained apologetically, "some interpretations must be made if those provisions are to make sense and to be understandable to those covered".

In November 1965, sixteen months after passage of the 1964 Civil Rights Act and four months after it went into effect, the EEOC finally issued full guidelines on sex discrimination under Title VII; the business community's fears were assuaged. The commission reiterated that it had received no help from the legislative history of the amendment; state laws, it said, constituted particularly difficult problems, but it did not believe that Congress intended to disturb laws that protected women against hazard or exploitation. The commission therefore stated that it would not consider the necessity to pay women minimum wages or premium wages for overtime as valid reasons for discriminating against women, and where the law permitted administrative exemption from state hours laws employers would have to seek them. An employer would not be breaking the law, however, if he refused to hire a woman for a job from which she was barred by state statute. In a December letter to a member of the National Woman's party, commissioner Richard Graham explained: "There seems to be a widely held misconception that this Commission can or would overturn state protective legislation. This is not the case. . . . If there is a clear conflict between the laws, we would not ask that [an employer] violate the state law. Rather, we would suggest that this conflict be brought to the attention of the Governor or the State Legislature or the state commission for remedy." In any case, the woman herself could bring suit, and the courts might render a judgement that essentially overturned state law. At a press conference on the new guidelines, commission chairman Franklin D. Roosevelt, Jr., assured the public that the guidelines would not result in a massive assault on sex segregated jobs. Four months later, the *New York Times* quoted a commission spokesperson as saying that the EEOC had moved cautiously on sex discrimination because of the lack of legal precedent, because of a concern for protective labour legislation, and because "it did not want this area to interfere with its man concern, racial discrimination."

The following month, April 1966, the commission once again evinced its half hearted commitment to enforcing the prohibition of sex-dissemination. It yielded to pressure from advertisers and newspapers who had already breached the original ruling on want ads by tailing to print the disclaimer of discrimination. Ignoring the recommendations of the ICSW and the CACSW, the Equal Employment Opportunity Commission amended its regulations to permit the placement of job notices in sex-segregated columns without any restriction, except that the administration itself could not state a preference. Commission vice-chair Luther Holcomb (now acting chairman since the resignation of Franklin Roosevelt. Jr., to run for governor of New York) believed that aggressive action on the part of the EEOC would hurt President Johnson's reputation. His judgement, combined with pressure from the newspaper industry, prevailed. Executive director Edelsberg explained the commission's action by observing that the sex amendment was a "fluke" "conceived out of wedlock." Esther Peterson warned Secretary Wirtz that interested women's groups might "react strongly to the abandonment of any attempt by the EEOC to enforce the sex-segregated advertisement ban of Title VII." Peterson herself asserted that "any rationale for this action on the part of the Commission is difficult to perceive."

Peterson's prediction that the EEOC action would inspire protest proved correct. In June Martha Griffiths, one of the prime movers behind the sex amendment to title VII, took to the House floor to blast the commission's decision. Griffiths accused the EEOC of a "wholly negative attitude" towards the sex provision, observing that it focused on ridiculous examples such as Playboy bunnies and male housemothers of college sororities. It had reached a "peak of contempt", she said, with the issuance of the ruling permitting sex-segregated want ads. This interpretation, Griffiths contended, bespoke on the part of the EEOC "nothing more than arbitrary arrogance, disregard of law, and a manifestation of flat hostility to the human rights of women.

Convinced of the power of Griffith's speech, Catherine East saw an opportunity to build support to change the EEOC's attitude. The third meeting of delegates from state commissions around the country was about to take place, planned by the CACSW. East arranged for copies of Griffith's speech to be distributed to the participants.

Although she was proud of the accomplishments of the President's Commission on the Status of Women and of the CACSW, East recognised that the ability of these bodies to make major changes was limited by their identification with the administration in power. East and her colleagues who had worked in the government had been looking for an outside group to take the lead and force the EEOC to respond seriously to the issue of sex discrimination in employment. The members of the state commissions arriving in Washington had been primed. The moment had arrived.

8

A New Women's Movement

In October 1966, three years to the month after the President's Commission on the Status of Women presented its report to John Kennedy, the first avowedly feminist organisation to emerge since suffrage held its inaugural conference. With the appearance of the National Organisation for Women, women leaders outside of government, building upon the president's Commission's report, took over the creation of the policy agenda for women from those in government who had served as "midwives of the Women's Movement." The new movement adopted the objectives of the activists who had laid the groundwork, but it went beyond their work in a signal wav. The women's movement of the 1960s forged a new, coherent, feminist philosophy that would enable women finally to make a claim for complete equality both in and outside the home.

The Creation of the National Organisation for Women

Martha Griffiths was not alone in her indignation at the behaviour of the EEOC. Although initially disturbed by the threat to protective labour laws Title VII represented, by 1966, virtually every women's organisation protested the EEOG's cavalier attitude toward sex discrimination. By June, a "proto-feminist" nucleus in Washington (Peterson, Catherine East, Mary Eastwood, and EEOC commissioner Richard Graham) had come to believe that the EEOC would not improve unless outside pressure from organised women served to heighten the commissioners' interest in enforcing the sex provision of Title VII. This cadre had begun to work toward the formation of a new outside group devoted exclusively to sex discrimination, starting with the traditional women's associations of the Women's Bureau coalition. These groups were reluctant, however, to establish an activist group that would fight exclusively for women's rights; as council member Viola Hymes had earlier explained, women's organisations hesitated to take the lead in the fight "for fear it would be interpreted that they were favouring women instead of looking upon everyone as having equal opportunity.

But other, less familiar, avenues were being explored. Betty Friedan, author of *The Feminist Mystique*, who had begun work on a book concerning the new law on sex discrimination, was now in close touch with Catherine East, Sonia Pressman, Pauli Murray, and Martha Griffiths—part of what Friedan later described as the "feminist underground" in Washington. Pressman, an attorney at the EEOC, told Friedan that only she could start a national organisation to fight for women as the civil rights movement had for blacks. Richard Graham, too, urged Friedan on, telling her that he had asked the mainstream women's associations, such as the League of Women Voters and the American Association of University Women, to develop such an organisation, but they had declined. Friedan nevertheless delayed. Although East and Eastwood supplied her with lists of women likely to be sympathetic, Friedan suggested that the state commissions on the status of women take the lead. East protested that women on the state commissions were too dependent on the state governors and had too little power of their own. Over Mary Keyserling's objections, East invited

Friedan to attend the Washington gathering of the state commissions in June.

Friedan took the opportunity the conference provided to probe the sentiments of the state commission members. Shortly before the meeting Friedan, to her dismay, had learned through her Washington friends that Lyndon Johnson did not intend to reappoint Richard Graham to the EEOC after his initial term expired in July. (Ironically, Graham himself had no sense that he was being "dismissed" from the commission, although he was aware that Roosevelt, Holcomb and Edelsberg preferred that he not be reappointed. Graham's term on the EEOC had ended; he welcomed the White House offer of the post of director of the National Teacher Corps as a chance to work effectively for civil rights free of the energy-draining backbiting of the EEOC. He left the EEOC unaware of the controversy swirling around his departure.) Mindful of East's words, Friedan invited a group of interested women participating in the state commission conference to come to her hotel room and discuss what could be done about Graham's reappointment and about the recent EEOC ruling regarding sex-segregated advertising. The women who caucused in Friedan's room agreed that a civil rights organisation for women was not necessary but proposed that a resolution be offered at the conference supporting Graham and insisting on better enforcement efforts by the EEOC. Kathryn Clarenbach, chairman of the Wisconsin commission on women and known for her close working relationship with the CACSW, volunteered to speak to Peterson, Keyserling, and Hickey about the proposal.

Administration officials had anticipated some expression of irritation at the conference. Esther Peterson confided to John Macy that "95 percent" of the delegates believed that the EEOC was lax about enforcing the sex provision of Title VII. Moreover, she said, a grapevine made up of "women active in women's groups, unions, civil rights groups and political parties" was communicating dissatisfaction because Lyndon Johnson's campaign to bring more women into government had lapsed.

But despite Peterson's obvious sympathy with the grievances, the action she and the other conference hosts took to address them brought the annoyance to a head. When Clarenback conferred with Hickey, Keyserling, and Peterson about offering resolutions on the subject, all three told her it could not be done because the conference participants were not official delegates and because conference organisers did not want resolutions critical of the administration emerging from a federally supported gathering. Angered by the ruling, Clarenbach reported back to Friedan and the others. Having had their request for action denied, the fifteen women who had met in Friedan's room the night before took over two tables at the conference luncheon. Within sight of the conference directors, Friedan, Clarenbach, and their colleagues planned an inaugural meeting for a new women's association. Friedan scribbled the name on a paper napkin: NOW—the National Organisation for Women.

In addition, disregarding the official decree, eighty representatives in the Title VII workshop voted for a resolution asking Lyndon Johnson to reappoint Richard Graham. Olya Margolin of the National Council of Jewish Women reported to AFL-CIO lobbyist Andrew Biemiller that "the most unfortunate part of these proceedings" was that some labour women joined conference participants ("equal-righters") in an attack on protective labour legislation, which "created the impression that labour is either divided or no longer concerned about these labour standards." Mary Keyserling ignored the disputes and the ire of conference participants. She reported to Secretary Writz that the conference had been "very successful", mentioning no disagreement of any kind.

Keyserling tried to pretend that nothing had happened, but the June conference constituted a crucial point in the history of women in the 1960s. Until then, either influential individuals or official government bodies had created a federal agenda for women and moved with caution and deference to traditional views about women, carefully couching requests for specific improvements in the language of liberal ideals and obeisance to women's "natural" roles as wife and mother. The formation of NOW indicated that many women were no longer satisfied working within the constraints imposed by being official members of governments. From that time forward, the federal government would no longer control or restrain the agenda of the women's movement; NOW could take action, as official groups could not, without executive sanction. At the conclusion of the June conference, NOW officers sent telegrams to Lyndon Johnson asking him to reappoint Richard Graham to the commission and requesting the EEOC to revise its ruling on sex-segregated want ads.

The target of NOW's original animus, the EEOC, was in extremis as the new group got underway. The *Chicago Tribune* alleged that Franklin Roosevelt, Jr., when he resigned in May 1966, had been "driven" from the commission over the issue of enforcing the sex provision of the civil rights law. In June commissioner Aileen Hernandez complained to the White House about the slowness in naming commission replacements and about the high staff turnover. Johnson did not fill Graham's post promptly; thus, in July the commission, with only three members, was at 60 percent of its total strength. The White House, concerned about the controversy over the commission and its personnel, decided to take no note of the July anniversary of the enactment of the civil rights statute.

The situation continued to decline. In August the EEOC issued a new ruling backing away from a position in support of protective labour laws, saying that it would not make decisions in cases of alleged conflict but would wait for court interpretations. In doing so, the commission now drew the wrath of labour women as well as ERA advocates. In September Hernandez sent a memorandum to the commission and its staff expressing her dismay at the long time lag in responding to complaints and at the neglect of sex discrimination. This grievance had no effect, however, and in October Hernandez submitted her resignation in disgust, effective November 10. Stephen Shulman, whom Johnson appointed to head the commission in September, was not in an enviable position. The National Organisation for Women intended to make sure he took his new job seriously.

An Outside Pressure Group

The new women's rights organisation convened its inaugural conference in October 1966, the first formal expression of the new wave of feminism. At the meeting, the membership elected Friedan president and Clarenbach, in absentia, chairman of the board; former EEOC commissioners Aileen Hernandez and Richard Graham both became vice-presidents. The composition of the board of directors disclosed NOW's origins in the discontent of elite women and their male supporters. The board included seven university professors or administrators, five state or national labour union officials, four federal or local government officials, four business executives, four members with some affiliation to a state commission on women, one physician, and three members of religious orders. Thanks to the media experience of the professionals in the organisation, the October conference elicited a surprising amount of press attention, which greatly enhanced NOW's impact from its birth.

Although NOW appeared because its founders grew impatient with the timid posture of ICSW and CACSW officials in relation to the Equal Employment Opportunity Commission, the formation of NOW did not imply a renunciation of the President's Commission on the Status of Women or of the ongoing groups created at the commission's request to implement its recommendations. Rather, the originators of the new organisation were motivated by an understanding of the intrinsic limitations of federal bodies. In the invitation to join the new organisation, the creators paid respects to the president's commission, the governors' commissions, the CACSW, and the ICSW as part of the "basis" laid "for realising the democratic goal of full participation and equal partnership for all citizens." And in the statement of purpose, adopted at the October meeting, they stated: "The excellent reports of the President's

Commission on the Status of Women and of the State Commissions have not been fully implemented. . . . They have no power to enforce their recommendations. . . . The reports of these Commissions have, however, created a basis upon which it is now possible to build." The architects of NOW established the organisation in order to commence "a civil rights movement for women" that would confront law and custom "to win for women the final right to be fully free and equal human beings." Although upset by the decision of Peterson, Keyserling, and Hickey not to permit a resolution at the conference, NOW's founders held no grudge against the administration officials concerned with women Friedan later referred to Esther Peterson and Eleanor Roosevelt as the "two towering figures of recent history", who had first brought together many of the new organisations' founders in the President's Commission on the Status of Women.

Likewise, Peterson bore no ill will toward the organisation that was preparing to wrest control of women's policy from the administration groups. In a memorandum to Civil Service Commission chairman John Macy, she described the membership list of the new organisation as "very distinguished", although she found its positions "rather militant". Their governing principle, she wrote, was that sex and race discrimination were intertwined (many had been active in the civil rights movement) and that the EEOC had proved consistently inadequate in righting these injustices. Moreover, the particular incidents leading to the group's formation were irrelevant; it was "inevitable" that some such organisation would appear. "The society", Peterson said, "simply is not going to take women and their needs seriously until women take themselves and their needs seriously enough to fight for them. . . . An organisation is needed to focus the underlying resentment and frustration into constructive channels. If NOW does not succeed, some other organisation will take its place".

Although Peterson characterised NOW's positions as "militant," in its first months NOW's programme closely paralleled the programme of the president's commission. In subsequent years NOW continued to owe to the president's commission its penchant for seeking federal action to ameliorate women's problems, its emphasis on employment issues, and its attractiveness for middle-class women who had first been sensitised to women's issues by the reports of the national and state commissions. As "targets for action" in the first year, NOW highlighted equal employment opportunity and the actions the federal government could take toward that end, including amendment of Executive Order 11246, which prohibited federal contractors from discriminating on the basis of race. It also focused on full deductability of childcare expenses, greater enforcement powers for the EEOC, the appointment of the full number of commissioners, revision of the regulations concerning advertising, and equal attention to the needs of minority women in federal poverty programmes. The agenda was very broad and included economic rights for homemakers, training programmes for mothers reentering the labour force, projects to address discrimination in educational institutions, prohibition of distinctions based on sex in jury service, and equal protection for women under the Constitution. The people who founded NOW were friends or colleagues of members of the presidential commission, or members themselves, and they agreed generally with the commission on many of the most pressing problems and their solutions.

As with the president's commission, NOW's founders did not raise questions concerning sexual freedom. In 1966 NOW did not mention homosexuality, and a statement that women should control their own reproduction was excised from the statement of purpose as being "too controversial." NOW's creators assumed that women would continue to live in traditional families, and they did not envision or endorse a radical restructuring of most institutions.

Similarly, in its founding year NOW approved the presidential commission's proposal regarding constitutional equality. Upon hearing of NOW's formation, the National

Woman's party, hoping for an ally, wrote immediately asking for the organisation's statement in favour of the Equal Rights Amendment. Mary Eastwood, who had been technical secretary of the PCSW Committee on Civil and Political Rights, which had formulated the commission's stance, wrote on NOW's behalf to the NWP that the ERA amendment was superfluous because the Constitution, properly interpreted, would guarantee equality without disturbing state labour laws.

But if NOW considered the PCSW a model in many ways, it also differed from the governmental bodies that preceded it in two significant respects. First, unlike the presidential commission, NOW was independent of traditional political structures and owed no allegiance to a party or politician. Rather than seeking to praise members of the administration, NOW warned that "official pronouncements of the advance in the status of women hide not only the reality of [a] dangerous decline, but the fact that nothing is being done to stop it." NOW pledged to prevent the election of any public official "who betrays or ignores the principle of full equality between the sexes" by mobilising the votes of feminist men and women. Since membership in NOW did not depend on the good favour of president or governor, NOW's freedom of action had few limits. It could afford to be, to use Peterson's term, "militant."

Second, and more important, NOW declined to share the presidential commission's view that sex roles were immutable. In its statement of purpose, the organisation's founders declared: "We reject the current assumptions that a man must carry the sole burden of supporting himself, his wife and family . . . or that marriage, home and family are primarily woman's world and responsibility—hers, to dominate—his to support. We believe that a true partnership between the sexes demands a different concept of marriage, an equitable sharing of the responsibilities of home and children and of the economic burdens of their support."

This renunciation of biological destiny ultimately permitted NOW to demand a kind of equality for women that neither the president's commission nor any other women's group preceding NOW could have claimed. For the first time, women seeking equal rights for women could offer a coherent and logical programme, founded on an internally consistent philosophy. Women could insist on equal treatment in the workplace because fathers, too, had the responsibility to take care of children. With this theoretical leap of great consequence, the feminists in NOW anticipated, rather than reflected, the prevailing viewpoint.

Still, despite its assertion of independence, in its initial overtures to federal officials NOW assumed a very respectful attitude. Soon after the organising conference, letters went out to the president, the attorney general, the chairman of the Civil Service Commission and the EEOC commissioners, courteously introducing the organisation. Emphasising NOW's interest in the administration of Title VII, the officers told the president: "Our greatest concern today is that the Equal Employment Opportunity Commission should be able and willing to fulfil its legal mandate to enforce the prohibitions against discrimination in employment based upon sex." But NOW also asserted the need for the appointment of women to government posts, affirmative action programs for women, and the inclusion of women in legislation and executive orders respecting racial discrimination. The officers expressed to the president their gratitude for his "past efforts."

Administration officials recognised immediately the significance of a new organisation dedicated to fighting for women's rights. In November, Civil Service Commission chief John Macy and three EEOC commissioners met with NOW officials to discuss the points. NOW raised in its letter EEOC chair Stephen Shulman indicated to correspondents that he was aware of NOW's position on the matters under discussion. The Department to Labour, also the recipient of a letter from NOW, congratulated the officers on NOW's objectives, which the secretary said the ICSW shared. Willard Wirtz wrote: "It is my hope that many of the advances you point to as needed can be effected." Esther Peterson promised her support: "Your organisation will be very useful at this moment and I am sure you know I am following it with great interest and will be helpful in any way I can.

The White House reacted more guardedly. The letter to the president went to Peterson with a request that she handle it, and Shulman counselled the president not to meet with NOW's officers, advising him that the EEOC commissioners had already done so. He suggested that the president wait a year to see "whether or not they have achieved a status worthy of Presidential attention.

NOW did not anticipate immediate results from the president. The group's founders recognised that the elimination of entrenched sex discrimination required a long-term educational and activist effort. "Our first order of business," Betty Friedan explained, "was to make clear to Washington, to employers, to unions and to the nation that someone *was* watching, someone *cared* about ending sex discrimination." The first goal of the organisation was publicity. Many NOW actions, such as picketing newspapers and integrating men's bars, had as their rationale simply the desire for media attention to make their presence known. This goal was easily achieved: from the moment of its birth, Washington politicians knew NOW was there.

Presidential acknowledgement come quickly, in fact. In March 1967 an aide advised the organisation's officers that the president found their recommendations "most welcome" and that in keeping with one of their proposals he was willing to amend the executive order prohibiting racial discrimination in federal employment and contractors to include sex discrimination.

Johnson's letter reflected the culmination of a series of developments. The President had issued EO 11246, which required affirmative action programmes to ensure equal opportunity for all races, in September 1965. By that time, Congress had already passed the Civil Rights Act, which prohibited sex discrimination in employment, and Esther

Peterson had warned that the omission of sex in the executive order "might prove embarrassing to the President." Furthermore, she argued, if left out then, it would create serious problems with women's organisations; it would have to be added eventually. Secretary Wirtz had disagreed. He cautioned Peterson that it was not the "moment in history" to press the point and that for her to do so would be "counter-productive." Peterson, outranked by Wirtz, had no choice but to desist, but the following spring the National Federation of Business and Professional Women's Clubs wrote to the White House to ask that sex discrimination be included in the executive order. In February 1967 the CACSW too asked for the addition of sex to EO 11246, and in March these organisations were joined by the Federal Women's Award Study Group, constituting the thirty-six winners since 1960, whom Johnson had also asked for recommendations. As support for the change grew, Peterson turned out to be right; Johnson asked the ICSW to recommend the form of the new executive order. With relatively little discussion, the ICSW advised the president simply to amend the original order to add the word *sex* wherever the phrase "race, creed, colour or national origin" appeared. This he did in October 1967. The dispute over whether sex discrimination should be treated like racial bias had ended. Because the executive order mandated positive action against discrimination on the part of the government, Civil Service Commission chief John Macy instituted the Federal Women's Programme, which was designed to upgrade efforts to improve women's position in the civil service. NOW president Betty Friedan claimed credit for the new amendment. The discussion of sex discrimination, Friedan declared, was "out in the clear light of day."

The cordial relationship between the new organisation and the federal bodies concerned with women's status quickly became problematical with the continued equivocation of the EEOC on protective labour legislation. Initially, NOW's founders themselves had no unified position. Pauli Murray and Mary Eastwood had come to the conclusion, argued in their landmark article, "Jane Crow and the Law", in the December 1965 issue of the *George Washington Law Review*, that laws for women alone had "waning utility." Kathryn Clarenbach, in contrast, continued to support the position espoused by Mary Keyserling and the Women's Bureau coalition that the EEOC should not overrule protective labour laws. But when a California woman filed a complaint with the EEOC against a firm that refused to promote her because of the state's maximum hours laws, and the commission declined to rule, NOW offered the woman its assistance in getting the California law nullified. Peterson suggested that the Department of Labour take a public position in favour of the plaintiff, as NOW requested; Keyserling, backed by the National Consumers League and the other members of the Women's Bureau coalition, urged the secretary not to intervene. Secretary Wirtz sided once again with Keyserling.

But the administration position on the issue of protective labour legislation could no longer be addressed and decided only "in house." NOW's membership grew rapidly—one year after its creation it counted twelve hundred members, with chapters in several states—but its influence continuously outstripped its actual numbers. Access to media and legal services made NOW a force to be reckoned with from the beginning. Thus, in 1967 the EEOC felt enough pressure that it held hearings on several issues pertinent to the women's cause, including protective labour legislation, age discrimination against airline stewardesses, who also customarily lost their jobs on marriage, help-wanted ads, and pension inequality.

NOW testified at the EEOC hearings against protective labour legislation, in company with Representative Martha Griffiths and representatives of the BPW and the United Automobile Workers, and together they succeeded in bringing about a change unwelcome to die-hard advocates of differential treatment for women. Katherine Ellickson spoke for the National Consumers League asking, along with some state labour officials, that the EEOC safeguard laws for women. But in

February 1968, the commission overturned its 1966 decision to leave the judgement entirely to the courts or to states for reconciliation, and it announced it would consider the arguments on a case-by-case basis. Labour unions objected again; the Amalgamated Clothing Workers called this application of Title VII "a modern version of the effort years ago to use the so-called Equal Rights Amendment . . . to deprive women workers of the protection of this legislation." Yet as more and more groups, from NOW to state commissions to labour unions, began to endorse the position that state labour laws applying only to women did more harm than good, the advocates of special treatment became increasingly isolated, outside the mainstream.

Despite the continuation of this historic controversy among seekers of women's rights, more often than not all the groups proved to be allied on the same side of most issues, continuing in the path of the president's commission by refusing to let the differences occupy centre stage. Four members of the CACSW, including Richard Lester who had been vice-chair of the presidential commission, signed NOW's petition to the EEOC to revise the ruling on job advertisements; the ICSW submitted a memorandum in support, as well as one contending that the airline industry's practice of firing stewardesses who married or who had reached the age of thirty-two constituted sex discrimination, a position NOW emphatically shared. The EEOC finally ruled in favour of the stewardesses in June 1968.

Forcing a change in the want ads position proved more difficult. In December 1967 the EEOC became the target of the first feminist demonstration in five decades when NOW set up picket lines in front of EEOC offices in five cities. Still, the commission remained obdurate. In February, Marguerite Rawalt, a member of the President's Commission on the Status of Women and the Citizens' Advisory Council on the Status of Women, and now general counsel for the National Organisation for Women, filed a mandamus suit in U.S. district court against the commission; the court agreed to dismiss the case only after the commission promised to improve its performance on behalf of women. Finally, in August, the EEOC promulgated the sought-after regulation that barred employers from advertising in sex-segregated newspaper columns. Fortas's prediction notwithstanding, the Supreme Court upheld the regulation in a 1973 decision, ruling that the First Amendment does not extend fully to commercial speech.

The issues raised by the EEOC's enforcement of Title VII of the 1964 Civil Rights Act dominated NOW's earliest days but did not consume them entirely. Once a clear position on protective labour legislation had been arrived at within the organisation, NOW's endorsement of the Equal Rights Amendment followed quickly. The effort to find a good court case to test the Fourteenth Amendment strategy had come to nothing, done in partly by the decisions on protective labour laws and partly by disinterest. Many who had been persuaded by the argument that women were protected by the Fourteenth Amendment now reconsidered. Although the National Woman's party had been bitterly disappointed by NOW's initial reluctance, an NWP member organised the D.C. branch of the new group and soon won the chapter's approval of the amendment. At the 1967 national conference, NOW decided to back the ERA by a vote of eighty-two to three, with twelve abstentions. The vote cost NOW the clerical services provided by NOW members who were affiliated with the Women's Division of the UAW, which at the time still opposed the ERA (the union reversed its stand two years later). Following the vote, NOW turned immediately to the NWP. One member wrote to ask Alice Paul for a list of congressional supporters and expressed her thanks "for your patient years of striving while most of the nation's women were asleep." Carl Hayden and Emanuel Celler, unimpressed by the new movement, continued to stymie congressional action. Feminists did not succeed in freeing the ERA from the House Judiciary Committee until 1970.

Despite its conversion to the amendment, NOW's insistence on a broad programme of women's rights distinguished its method of operation from the one-issue approach of the National Women's party. Alice Paul's pleasure with NOW's advocacy of the ERA was therefore restrained. She took particular exception to NOW's 1967 endorsement of the movement to repeal abortion laws in recognition of women's right to control their own bodies. Paul contended that taking positions on such issues as abortion "gets the men all mixed up." NOW, interested in achieving equality and autonomy for women in every area of American life, as well as in drawing large numbers of women and men into the movement, saw no purpose to narrowing its focus. Still, it considered the ERA to be of major importance.

The growing interest in the Equal Rights Amendment, as evidenced by the support of NOW and a renewed commitment by the BPW and the General Federation of Women's Clubs, did not sway the CACSW. Member Marguerite Rawalt, the one PCSW member in favour of the ERA, asked that the council reconsider its position, but it declined. Catherine East told Esther Peterson that the delay in the Supreme Court case the president's commission had recommended and the negative attitude of the courts with respect to decisions under Title VII accounted for at least part of the new interest in the amendment. Rather than champion the ERA, Peterson urged the Justice Department to find a good test case. The administration maintained this position to the end, but it was soon to be in the minority on the issue.

The 1968 presidential campaign took place in the midst of turmoil over racism, urban riots, the war in Vietnam, and paralysing student demonstrations. The assassinations that year of Martin Luther King, Jr., in April and Robert Kennedy in June, the Poor People's Campaign" in Washington in the spring, and the violent clashes between peace marchers and the police at the Democratic National Convention in Chicago all highlighted and focused the impulse toward social reform. The just-emerging women's movement was a small part of that tableau, but even so, women's issues were achieving a new salience.

In the 1968 campaign, both NOW and the National

Woman's party urged all the candidates to speak on behalf of the ERA, and most did. During the New Hampshire primary Eugene McCarthy, the amendment's chief sponsor and challenger of Lyndon Johnson for the Democratic party's nomination, highlighted his support for the amendment in his campaign literature and in a special mailing to the New Hampshire Federation of Women's Clubs. Hubert Humphrey, calling the Era a "vital issue," reminded amendment advocates of his allegiance while in the Senate. American party candidate George Wallace favoured the ERA, as many conservatives always had, and held up his wife, Lurleen, as one who contributed to women's advancement in her role as governor of Alabama. Richard Nixon again affirmed his long-standing approval. Senator Robert Kennedy as less enthusiastic; he promised support only if other measures proved inadequate. Unlike the National Women's party, however, the National Organisation for Women asked the candidates to express themselves as well on a whole variety of women's issues. For the first time in four decades, a genuine national women's movement was bringing a wide array of issues to the attention of a national audience.

A chain of events accounted for the appearance of the first new feminist organisation of the 1960s. The civil rights movement served as the vanguard, its philosophy, tactics, and successes priming the political and social environment and providing models for action. The changing configuration and providing models for action. The changing configuration of women's work lives and their now-established place in the workforce produced a disjuncture between women's lives as they were living them and the social setting that offered few supports, either ideological or material. The formation of the President's Commission on the Status of Women in 1961, in recognition of this disjuncture, had resulted in the creation of a national network of knowledgeable women concerned about their status. In 1964, the proponents of the ERA accomplished a legislative coup with the enactment of a federal law that barred sex discrimination in employment. The statute had problematical implications for the Women's Bureau coalition, but the derision exhibited by the Equal Employment Opportunity Commission, the agency responsible for enforcing the law, angered the national network of women newly sensitised to inequities confronting women. Indeed, the commission's behaviour spurred the women into establishing a new association committed to fighting for women's rights. Inaugurated by women affiliated with the president's commission and the resulting state commissions, the National Organisation for Women reflected both the commission's successes in bringing the status of women to the fore and their limitations in taking effective action to improve it. NOW's creation bespoke as well the short reach of the narrowly focused, ingrown movement for the Equal Rights Amendment and expressed the frustration of politically sensitive women relegated to token appointments.

After the formation of NOW, federal policy makers had to start responding to demands sustained by a high degree of public awareness rather than initiating moderate actions in the relative calm of general disinterest. The recommendations of the president's commission and the citizens' advisory council, the existence of the state commissions on women, the efforts of mainstream women's organisations, the activity of the National Women's party, the inclusion in Title VII of sex as a prohibited basis for employment discrimination, the work of women representatives to Congress and of women within the executive branch, and NOW's overt feminist agenda became intermingled as influences on the development of federal policy, with synergistic effect. Unquestionably, by the end of Lyndon Johnson's term the federal government faced demands and expectations concerning women undreamt of at the time of John Kennedy's inauguration.

Moreover, yet another strain of active feminism emerged at the end of the decade, with the appearance of women's groups on the community level growing out of the antiwar struggle and the movement for social justice. In the fall of 1967 local women's liberation groups began to appear in several cities, as radical women recognised the futility of reform within New Left civil rights and community action organisations. Younger than the women who had formed NOW and committed to local, rather than national, activity, these small, autonomous groups developed a technique of uncovering the political nature of the oppression of women through candid discussion of women's personal lives.

"Consciousness raising" became the initiation rite of the women's movement; locally focused groups went from there to organising day-care centres, rape crisis committees, women's health collectives, and a plethora of movement publications. By the mid seventies, women involved in these groups had begun to seek state and federal support for local programmes, forming coalitions with staid feminist organisations such as NOW. And NOW, which had started life as a top-heavy lobbying group, itself encouraged the emergence of local chapters. The branches of the women's movement, in their essential parts, had merged. With forty thousand members in 1974, NOW offered a highly visible and respectable link to a national movement, but the diversity of smaller groups provided comfortable alternatives for almost any woman to join.

The women's movement ultimately forced federal policy makers to consider action to amerliorate the disadvantages women suffered in virtually every part of their lives. But the federal initiatives taken *before* the movement's rebirth played a crucial role in forming that movement; they broke a critical stalemate among women's organisations, set much of the early agenda, legitimated the idea of women fighting for their rights, provided legislative tools, and helped to establish a network of women nationwide who could be easily mobilised for the cause of women.

9

The Equal Rights Amendment and the Ambivalent Legacy of World War II

World War II put women into work they had never done before. Highly skilled and highly paid, women workers producing war materiel demonstrated that they could do virtually any job. The information proved unsettling. American tradition dictated that women, especially married women, keep house and raise children, not put rivets into airplane fuselages. The nation was at once grateful to its women for their help and unnerved at how well they performed. Women activists with political agendas of long standing sought to capitalise on the feelings of gratitude, proposing federal measures to protect women from discrimination. But they faced a resistance strengthened by the anxieties of wartime dislocation.

Postwar Backlash

The federal government had enticed women into the labour force for war work. Federal funds helped communities take care of the children, and the National War Labour Board promised equal pay with men, declaring wage differentials based on sex impermissible (partly to lure women to work and partly to keep wage rates up in preparation for the GIs' return). A massive public relations campaign sang the praises of "Rosie the Riveter." Magazine story writers began to portray married women workers favourably, able to handle their jobs competently while meeting their family responsibilities. Work and love went together—but only for the duration. Advertisers who included working moms in their ads made it clear that Mom was serving because it was her duty but that she would be home again full-time as soon as she could. Now, she had to take care of her kids not directly but by doing war work. As Maureen Honey describes it, "The role allocated to women in wartime propaganda, then, was a complicated mixture of strength and dependence, competence and vulnerability, egalitarianism and conservatism."

In response to patriotism and new opportunities, the female labour force swelled from thirteen million in 1940 to nineteen million and more in 1944. By March of that year, almost one-third of all women over the age of fourteen were in the labour force, and the numbers of women in industry had increased almost 500 per cent, to one woman worker in three. The opportunities created by the war allowed women to leave domestic service jobs: between 1940 and 1944 the percentage of working women who held domestic jobs dropped from 17.7 to only 9.5. Still, more than half of women who worked during the war held clerical, sales, service, or domestic jobs. These women did their duty, but they faced many burdens. The number of childcare facilities never approached the need, areas with military personnel lacked adequate schools, housing was scarce near military installations and defense plants, and few businesses adjusted hours to accommodate women workers.

Even with all these difficulties, however, policy makers were concerned that women in non-traditional jobs would not willingly relinquish them at the end of the war. As a result, government propaganda, midwar, did an about-face. Because the original exhortations to women to do war work had never challenged the core of ideas about femininity, because no one had suggested that work was more than a sacrifice women had willingly made for the most motherly of reasons, the shift was an easy one. The message was clear: although women *could* do anything, authentic women would choose to be home with their families. Women's magazines fell in line with the government's efforts and spotlighted articles on the importance of mothers caring for their children.

Public opinion polls, however, revealed that between 60 and 85 percent of women engaged in war work did not want to leave their non-traditional jobs at the end of the conflict. Out of anxiety that women workers might tenaciously hang on to their jobs, the federal government terminated daycare funding and gave veterans the right to displace wartime workers. The contraction of war material manufacturing alone displaced workers, male and female, without further ado. Within one month of V-J day, the government cancelled $35 billion worth of defense contracts. Employers also began now to revise their judgement of their women workers: in the postwar version of the tale, they had not been very good after all, prone to high absenteeism and "bad attitudes." Women's organisations of all stripes worked against the notion that employers should force women out of jobs, but to little avail.

Those women who had them lost their high-paying, highskilled jobs, but the attempt to get women out of the workforce entirely did not succeed. The dismantling of war industries merely occupations. Companies laid women off at a rate 75 percent greater than that for men, and the returning veterans reassumed the traditionally male jobs. The director of the Women's Bureau, Frieda Miller, suggested that women who had been laid off from the munitions industry look to the (lower-paying) service sector for employment—which, given no other options, they did. Thus, although 3.25 million women either quit or were fired during the period from September 1945 to November 1946, nearly 2.75 million women assumed jobs, making the net decline only 6000,000 women. But Rosie the Riveter had become a file clerk.

Practical considerations had dictated the ejection of women

from wartime employment: returning soldiers needed jobs. Americans worried about the return of the biting depression that had preceded the war. Then, jobs for "heads of households" had taken priority. Intense opposition to married women workers had resulted even in occasional legal bans against hiring them, and in some families in which the wife had been the sole wage earner husbands had suffered acute emotional distress. No one wished to contemplate the recurrence of such a phenomenon. In the twelve months following June 1945, nine million military personnel were discharged, and policy makers now sought to ensure that the former GIs would not be displaced by women from jobs they had a right to as "breadwinners." With the contraction of defense manufacturing, the economic dislocation of the postwar period added to the pervasive strain that had attended the war years.

But a still more insidious backlash emerged following the war, separate from the economic considerations resolved in part by women's relinquishing their jobs. As the psychiatrist Edwin Krause and the novelist Pearl Buck had both warned, by making them the beneficiaries of the heroic male warriors, the war caused a major setback for women. Popular literature counselled women to forget their own needs in order to make their beaux more comfortable, and articles advised them to cultivate feminine characteristics, eschewing the independence, assertiveness, and competency they had acquired from their experiences on the home front. Government planners had defined the major postwar domestic problem as the readjustment of sixteen million veterans, and they believed that readjustment would come sooner if the vets found their girls as they had left them, not as independent working women.

The anxiety of readjustment translated into a desire for the reinstitution of traditional family life supported by traditional sex roles. Everyone wanted to forget the trauma of the war, including the evidence that women could perform the work of men. A survey of women's roles as portrayed in magazine fiction in 1945 showed careers for women depicted more unsympathetically than since the turn of the century. Women themselves sought the peace and pleasures of marriage and motherhood. The marriage rate, which had averaged 121 per thousand during the war, peaked at 148 per thousand in 1946, and the median marriage age for women fell more than a year from 21.5 to 20.3. More than ever before, women were trying for both work and love. Pushed out of high-paying "men's jobs", they acquiesced to doing women's work at home and in the office.

Women Leaders and Women's Issues

One group of women—the small and elite cadre that composed the leadership of national women's organisations—recognised both the vulnerability that women workers laboured under and the possibility of doing something to ameliorate it. If World War II created a backlash that coerced women out of war jobs and into white-collar work, it also generated a felling of gratitude toward these women for the contribution they had made to the war effort, one no less essential than the military commitment. In October 1945, President Harry Truman offered them some recognition:

> Since the earliest days of settlement and the beginnings of this great Republic of ours, American women have built for themselves a proud record of achievement, of unselfish devotion to the public welfare, of courageous industry in advancing every good cause. And never have they done a more magnificent job than during the crisis of recent years, both as private citizens and responsible public officials. To the women of America, I say—your untiring efforts to speed the winning of the war, your tender care and skilled nursing of those struck down on the battlefield, your passionate belief in the possibility of a just and lasting peace, and your effective work in advancing that great cause, need no tribute from me to make them shine as one of the glorious pages in our history.

Women leaders hoped to capitalise on such gratitude to win at least some protection for the worker once heralded as "the woman behind the man behind the gun."

But these activists disagreed about the best goal to pursue a controversy already more than two decades old. The break among women's groups had taken place shortly after women, in 1920, won the right to vote. By 1945 the old suffrage coalition had split into three separate, though overlapping, interest groups, each with a different (but not necessarily incompatible) agenda determined by ideology and class identification: one group pursued legislation for working women, one sought an equal rights amendment to the Constitution and the third aimed at securing a more prominent place for women in political parties.

The first group had roots going back to the settlement movement of the 1890s and the Progressive-era push for protective labour legislation for women. Middle-class women concerned about the welfare of their underclass sisters working in factories had formed organisations to improve conditions for industrial labourers, in some cases joining forces with the women they hoped to help. These organisations—especially the National Women's Trade Union League and the National Consumers League—persuaded the federal government to undertake a massive study of working conditions of women and children, which was published in 1910. They used the data collected to promote state laws applying to women establishing minimum wages, maximum hours, weight restrictions on lifting, and prohibitions against night work. This effort to prevent employers from mercilessly exploiting women workers succeeded to some degree in nearly every state. Sustained by a liberal ideology of participation in government, active public intervention to assist those in need, and a firm belief in the American institutions of enlightened and regulated free enterprise, these reformers fought for suffrage as a means by which women could protect themselves and their families. This same group also persuaded federal administrators to establish a "Women in Industry Service" during World War I to protect women who entered defense work, and in 1920 Congress responded to pressure to make the new agency permanent: it became the Women's Bureau, located within the Department of Labour. With all players believing that both government and private industry would respond to demonstrated needs of workers, the bureau's function was restricted to the collection of information about women workers.

Yet the organisations that had been instrumental in creating the Women's Bureau looked to it to provide not only information but also leadership. In 1945 the "Women's Bureau coalition" (as it will be called in the following pages) included the following associations: the National Women's Trade Union League (which would disband in 1950), the National Consumers League, the Young Women's Christian Association, the National Council of Jewish Women, the National Council of Catholic Women, the National Council of Negro Women, the League of Women Voters (although the league became less interested in women's issues as the decade progressed), the American Association of University Women, and various women's affiliates of the American Federation of Labour and the Congress of Industrial Organisations. Not every organisation was involved in every issue, and other groups occasionally participated on specific matters, but in general it was these associations that the bureau staff most often consulted and that usually rallied to the Women's bureau positions. The coalition lacked key groups, however, especially major labour organisations and political clubs. Isolated from power centres both inside the government and outside and handicapped by a politically maladroit director, Mary Anderson (who headed the bureau for almost twenty-five years), the bureau had difficulty swaying policy makers.

During World War II, the Women's Bureau coalition had sought essentially to make sure that employers did not use the war emergency as a way of vitiating standards for women workers. At the end of the war, although they looked with some distress on the wholesale dispatch of the female labour force, these organisations agreed with the general goal that married women should be supported by their husbands, who would be earning decent salaries doing men's work. For the women who had to stay in the labour force, the coalition sought to maintain or expand laws regarding work hours and minimum wage protections.

The second group of women activists, smaller and more elite, grew out of the last stages of the suffrage fight in the 1910s, when it splintered from the National American Woman Suffrage Association (NAWSA), the group leading the battle for the vote in the mainstream liberal political tradition. Headed by Alice Paul, a charismatic militant suffragist, the National Woman's Party (NWP) used highly visible and inflammatory demonstrations to get suffrage on the front pages of the nation's newspapers. The more traditional-minded leadership of the NAWSA feared that such actions would hurt the cause by creating a backlash, but sheer rivalry also played a role in the antagonism between the two groups.

Friction appeared again early in the 1920s over Paul's decision to introduce an amendment to the Constitution to guarantee women complete legal equality with men. The Women's Bureau coalition objected that the amendment would decimate the protective labour laws they had worked so hard to obtain, thus leaving working women defenseless. The NWP was not unsympathetic; composed largely of women of wealth and unusual educational attainment and concerned chiefly about the right of women to work as professionals, it initially sought a compromise that would have excluded labour laws from the purview of the Equal Rights Amendment (ERA) it proposed. But these attempts proved futile, and the NWP ultimately took the position that laws only for women did more harm than good. The party argued variously that all labour laws should apply to both sexes or that labour laws were flat-out undesirable, the latter view reflecting the conservative political philosophy of many NWP members who opposed government interference in private enterprise. In 1928 the party endorsed the Republican Hoover-Curtis presidential ticket, primarily because Charles Curtis had been a sponsor of the ERA but also because many

NWP officers were Republicans. (Neither presidential candidate had announced in favour of the ERA, although the Democratic candidate, Al Smith, was certainly against it, being an ardent enthusiast of protective labour laws.)

Throughout the 1920s and 1930s, the NWP persuaded several women's organisations to support the ERA and to separate themselves from the advocates of protective legislation. By the 1940s, the National Federation of Business and Professional Women's Clubs (BPW), the General Federation of Women's Clubs, the National Association of Women Lawyers, the National Education Association, and various other smaller professional women's organisations had endorsed the Equal Rights Amendment and agreed to work with the NWP in pursuit of that goal.

But the NWP insisted on retaining leadership in the battle. Paul was not interested in a mass-based group; rather, she sought to create a Washington-based "elite vanguard," single-mindedly devoted to the pursuit of the Era and willing to follow her directions. The membership of the NWP endorsed her design. Almost all had participated in the suffrage battle, and the group made little attempt to recruit new members. By 1945 party membership—which, it claimed, had numbered ten thousand in the 1920s—had fallen to four thousand, even by its own highly inflated figures; only some six hundred paid annual dues. The party's intense devotion to its single cause did indeed make it influential out of proportion to its numbers.

Meanwhile, the NWP and the Women's Bureau Coalition had become archenemies. The Women's Bureau coalition continued to cooperate, if uneasily, with other pro-ERA organisations, like the BPW and the General Federation of Women's Clubs, on specific projects such as equal pay legislation; but after World War II the fight for the ERA constituted almost the entire programme of the National Woman's party, and its defeat the major consolidated effort of the Women's Bureau coalition.

A third group of political women held itself somewhat aloof

from this battle, pursuing a different goal. This contingent had appeared after the achievement of suffrage in 1920—in fact, in response to it. These women had become active in the national political parties' governing bodies, the Democratic National Committee (DNC) and the Republican National Committee (RNC), and they were committed to seeing that women quickly attained their share of power within these political structures. Moreover, they wanted women appointed to government positions because they believed both that women appointees would improve government and that appointments of women would potentially benefit all women. They were supported by women in state party organisations and by female journalists, who viewed the number of women political appointees as an index of an administration's interest in women's advancement. In the 1930s the political party women were indistinguishable from the Women's Bureau coalition, and both they and the ERA proponents opposed the discriminatory features of the National Recovery Administration codes and discrimination against women workers during the Great Depression. By the 1940s, however, political party women had gone one of two routes: either they openly espoused the Equal Rights Amendment, reflecting their own constituency of middle-class professional women, or else they simply tried to minimise potential fallout from the conflict by giving their party enough female appointments to counteract accusations of indifference to women's issues.

If class made a difference in support for the ERA, race apparently did not. Black women's organisations split over the amendment along the same lines white women's associations did. The National Association of Coloured Women, under the influence of Mary Church Terrell, a wealthy militant suffragist, endorsed the ERA, but the National Council of Negro Women, founded by Mary McLeod Bethune in 1935, voiced concern for protective labour legislation and in 1944 went on record opposing the amendment. One member warned against the council's being led astray by the promise of equal rights: "We are being rocked to sleep by a trick phrase—one dear to us as to other underprivileged groups, and therefore calculated to dull our ability for discriminating between what is good and what appears to be good."

Representatives from black women's organisations often took part in meetings arranged by the Women's Bureau coalition and were more visible fighting the amendment than favouring it. Many factors were at work here. The Women's Bureau coalition was more hospitable to black women than was the National Woman's party, which purposively narrowed its membership and its goals. The Women's Bureau coalition identified black women, as it did working women, as a special group requiring its assistance in the fight for economic opportunities. On some occasions, the white, middle-class women's organisations making up the Women's Bureau coalition even undertook to combat racism as a separate endeavour. Thus, black women felt more empathy from these white women. The NWP, in contrast, had no interest in civil rights for blacks, except when it could insist that women be included, for the sake of equity, in governmental measures aimed at racial discrimination. Further, the NWP, which accepted ERA proponents of all persuasions, had a wide tolerance for racists, and Paul herself frequently expressed racist sentiments. When convenient, the NWP used racist arguments to persuade Southerners to favour the ERA—that white women should not be denied rights accorded to black men. Such a ploy would hardly make the organisation appealing to black women.

But these considerations had a secondary role in determining black women's response to this struggle. Their position was clear: equal rights for women was a secondary issue; every black women's group considered the fight against racism its primary battle, more so since World War II, which had offered unprecedented opportunities for black women and men, as for white women. Black women were able to give up domestic jobs for higher-paying factory positions, and the number of black workers in government service more than tripled. War jobs encouraged blacks to move from rural areas in the South to Northern cities, and although the new mix of population often elicited antagonism, the economic benefits were significant. The clashes brought the endemic problem of racism once again to the foreground, however, as did the treatment of black men in the armed services. Blacks disproportionately joined the military, and discrimination there seemed scorchingly hypocritical in view of the fact that American troops were fighting German racial supremacists. In 1942, James Farmer founded the congress for Racial Equality; the National Association for the Advancement of Coloured People increased its membership nine-fold during the war.

The fight for civil rights for blacks and the struggle on behalf of women remained separate, however. Little overlap existed in the personnel engaged in these efforts, although both drew on the same liberal ideology. ERA supporters saw opportunities whenever the government appeared to move toward helping blacks, and both the Women's Bureau coalition and the National Woman's party found useful models for federal action in black activist strategies. But virtually everyone engaged in these efforts in the postwar period saw crucial distinctions between discrimination based on sex and that based on race.

All women activists shared the view that discrimination against women based on crude ideas of masculine superiority had to be eliminated, but the split between the ERA advocates and the Women's Bureau coalition itself reflected the general ambivalence toward women's roles. Both groups were trapped by the apparent verity that only women could care adequately for children. The Women's Bureau coalition tried to resolve the conflict between independence for women and motherhood; the NWP did not address it. The intensity of the disagreement between them came less from practical considerations than from the difference in the way each group handled this issue.

Although both sought to improve the way that women were treated in the public arena, the people associated with the Women's Bureau argued that women's special function in the world—to nurture families and society—ultimately took precedence over the need for individual opportunity. In their view, the American legal tradition rightly acknowledged the unique role of women by differentiation in the law. Ideally, this group believed, no married woman with small children would work. Rose Schneiderman of the National Women's Trade Union League had remarked in 1908 that women who wanted to work under the same conditions as men "might be putting their own brothers or sweethearts, or husbands out of a job." In establishing the Women's Bureau in 1920, Secretary of Labour William Wilson stated: "All will agree that women in industry would not exist in an ideal scheme." Although necessity sometimes forced women into industrial occupations, the Women's Bureau coalition judged such work to be inappropriate for women, and the state within its rights to limit female activity in this kind of employment.

Inside these boundaries, however, the Women's Bureau coalition sought to expand opportunities for women and to eradicate many forms of outright economic and legal discrimination. They advocated entrance into the professions on an equal basis with men and asserted that the state had an obligation to guarantee the right of women to be rewarded according to their merits. (They did not, however, concern themselves with the problems of women professionals, whom they believed could fend for themselves.)

The National Woman's party, conversely, believed that every public activity befitting men was acceptable for women and that, indeed, it was desirable for all women to have careers. The party did not view woman as frail, in need of special protection, and largely passed over the fact the most women worked in low-paying jobs and had neither the resources nor the education to become professionals. Since many in the NWP's leadership were conservatives who opposed statutory interference in private enterprise, they further contended that the ERA rendered any additional legislation for women unnecessary. Like the Women's Bureau coalition, the NWP considered childrearing a woman's task, but it did not address the problem of how a woman could reconcile motherhood and professional responsibilities. Many party members had simply chosen not to marry; others ran households with the assistance of paid help.

The internal contradictions within each group's philosophy, created by the intractable problem of childcare responsibility, undermined the possibility that either could succeed in gaining its objectives, even if the social setting were receptive, which it was not. The Women's Bureau coalition sought equal wages for women workers and access to higher-paying jobs, but at the same time it claimed a need for special protection for those workers. Employers quickly agreed that women workers needed special consideration, but they used that rationale to discriminate against them in wages and responsibility. For its part, the NWP asserted without convincing evidence that the ERA would eliminate the need for further legislation to give women equality of pay and job opportunity. The NWP took no account of extralegal causes of discrimination. So long as social norms decreed that women held the chief responsibility for childrearing and homemaking—a point the NWP did not contest—employers could justify differential treatment on the basis that a woman's commitment to work was limited as a man's was not. Thus, each plan of action addressed only a portion rather than the whole of the complex problem of women's status.

In the postwar period the argument over women's roles played itself out in Congress as well. The National Woman's party, advocating the Equal Rights Amendment, took the offensive, while the Women's Bureau coalition played defense.

The Equal Rights Amendment Ascendant, 1946

The battle over the Equal Rights Amendment dominated the politics of women's rights and opportunities in postwar Washington. Interested players either took sides in favour or against or else they ducked by supporting ostensibly neutral alternative measures that were in fact thinly disguised attempts to scuttle the amendment. But one way or the other, the ERA held centre stage. For both adherents and opponents, a bold question awaited decision, especially in the aftermath of women's wartime contribution: were women now to be viewed as autonomous individuals, or did they remain tied in a special way to the family, essentially dependent on the protection or both husband and state?

Shortly before the war, the ERA had made some significant progress. In July 1937, the National Federation of Business and Professional Women's Clubs, a prestigious organisation of politically active women numbering sixty-five thousand, established the ERA as a legislative priority. The following year, the Senate Judiciary Committee reported it, although without recommendation, to the floor of the Senate, the first time the amendment had reached the floor of either house since its introduction in 1923. It was quickly recommitted.

In May 1942 the Senate Judiciary Committee, under the leadership of chairman James Houghes (D-Del.) voted nine to three to report the amendment favourably and in 1943 the ERA was the first resolution introduced in the House, cosponsored by forty-two members. The Senate Judiciary Committee again approved it, twelve to four, in May 1943, with a request for early and favourable action. The original amendment considered in 1923 had read: "Men and women shall have equal rights throughout the United States and in every place subject to its jurisdiction"; in order to bring the language in line with the Nineteenth Amendment (granting women the right to suffrage), the Judiciary Committee adopted alternative wording provided by Alice Paul. The new proposed amendment ran: "Equality of rights under the law shall not be denied or abridged by the United States, or by any State, on account of sex." The House Judiciary Committee, after heavy lobbying by Catholic organisations committed to women's traditional roles, voted fifteen to eleven against reporting the ERA to the House, but proponents of the measure were increasingly hopeful that it would carry on a wave of wartime enthusiasm.

The amendment's advocates exploited the wartime esteem for the competent woman and stepped up their lobbying efforts. Alice Paul revamped the organisation of the National Woman's party and enlisted such luminaries as Mary Woolley, former president of Mount Holyoke College, the artist Georgia O'Keeffe, and the birth control reformer Margaret Sanger to stand up for the ERA. Other notable women also responded to Paul's entreaties: Pearl Buck, Helen Haves, Katharine Hepburn, Judge Sarah Hughes, Margaret Mead, and Congresswomen Margaret Chase Smith and Clare Borthe Luce.

The NWP kept itself a small, elite vanguard, but to benefit from the power of numbers it created an umbrella organisation, the Women's Joint Legislative Committee (WJLC). A coalition of all the organisations that endorsed the ERA, the combined membership of the WJLC totalled between five and six million members, a formidable constituency. The NWP orchestrated an intense lobbying campaign in Congress and within the political parties, dominating the movement for the ERA—sometimes to the annoyance of the other organisations involved. But if the NWP insisted on the authority, it also shouldered most of the administrative and financial burden.

The Women's Bureau led the counterattack. The ERA angered bureau director Mary Anderson, who had headed the bureau since its founding. Anderson had begun her working life in 1889, at age sixteen, as a stitcher in a shoe factory. By 1900 she had been elected president of her local, and in 1911 she gave up her factory job to become a full-time organiser. Devoted to laws protecting women workers, she viewed the ERA as an absurd theoretical pronouncement, unrelated to the realities of women's lives and natures. The bureau had been created to help women function as wives and mothers even if their economic circumstances drove them into the workforce; Anderson saw the defeat of the ERA as her first responsibility.

A legal treatise drawn up at her request by the solicitor of the Department of Labour, Douglas B. Maggs, became the department's fundamental position paper on the subject. It warned of injury to women as wives and mothers should the ERA be added to the Constitution. Ratification of the ERA, Maggs admonished, would unsettle the law for years. The extensive litigation would result, he was sure, in "highly undesirable" changes in the Social Security system; equal induction into the armed services; changes in workmen's compensation laws; upheaval in laws requiring husbands to support their families; and repeal of "reasonable protective legislation" with "consequent social loss." Moreover, Maggs argued, the attempt to extend such laws to men would render the statutes subject to constitutional attack. He concluded his paper by asserting that a constitutional amendment that would nullify statutory differences "having a reasonable and rational factual basis" would lead to "social and legal consequences which even the proponents of the proposal would deplore if they had the candour to recognise them." Maggs added in a footnote: "Fanatical adherence to a doctrinaire principle or dogma such as the theoretical equality of rights of men and women is foreign to the spirit of Anglo-American legislation and jurisprudence. If the proposal is ratified it should be regarded as an unwholesome original development in the law." His characterisation of the amendment's advocates as "fanatical" indicated accurately that the bureau did not foresee the possibility of compromise. Indeed, the two visions were irreconcilable.

When Frieda Miller assumed leadership of the Women's Bureau after Anderson's retirement in 1944, she pledged to continue the fight "with all the resources" at her command. Miller had begun her career in public service in 1929 under Governor Franklin D. Roosevelt, as head of New York State's Women in Industry Service. Before joining the government, Miller had worked in organisations concerned with the protection of working women, particularly the Women's Trade Union League. Her antipathy to the Equal Rights Amendment was therefore of long standing. Out in front on the issue, she called the amendment "radical, dangerous and irresponsible", its potential effects "calamitous."

Both she and other ERA opponents recognised, however, that they stood on vulnerable ground with only a negative campaign. Acknowledging that some laws did discriminate against women and that some labour statutes had outlived their utility, the bureau began to examine state codes. Its mission was to find laws that needed to be eliminated and to identify those that continued to protect women but that would be at risk under the ERA. The bureau uncovered several categories of laws it defined as harmful to women; many limited the right of married women to own and convey property, to make contracts, to establish domicile, to control bequests, and to exercise parental authority. The bureau recommended that state legislatures repeal these statutes.

The National Woman's party contended that elimination of laws one by one would take too long. It also attacked as a limitation on women's freedom such regulations as laws restricting work hours for women. Good labour laws should be extended to both sexes, the NWP insisted, bad ones simply expunged. In response to the bureau assertion that the Fourteenth Amendment prohibited "unreasonable" laws, the NWP pointed out correctly that the Supreme Court had never interpreted the Fourteenth Amendment to prohibit discrimination against women.

The momentum seemed to be with the National Woman's party and its wealthy, influential, single-minded members. In 1944 the Republican National Convention included a plank supporting the ERA, as it had in 1940. Indeed, from its inception enthusiasm for the amendment had been stronger among Republicans, and the argument that protective labour legislation would be affected won less sympathy from probusiness Republicans than from liberal Democrats. In 1940 representatives of the League of Women Voters, who had lobbied against the proposal in the platform committee, had dubbed its inclusion "the shock of the century", and a reporter for the *New York Times* had called the argument "the most extensive and portentous feminine controversy in the history of the country".

Now in 1944, however, the right over the Democratic platform resulted in victory for ERA advocates as well. The Democrats, too, saw women earning a place for themselves as independent individuals and needed to encourage that position—at least for the duration of the war. Eleanor Roosevelt failed to speak against the amendment as she had in 1940, citing the confusion of the war and the uncertainties of the peace. It was difficult to argue in favour of labour legislation to limit women's hours when men were dying on foreign battlefields. The Democrats also felt the pressure of the Republican pronouncement. Were Democrats less committed to equality for women? The general disorganisation of the opposition allowed ERA supporters, among them Perle Mesta and Emma Guffey Miller, a Democratic committee-woman from Pennsylvania and the sister of Senator Joseph Guffey, successfully to capitalise on women's war efforts. The Democratic plank finally read: "We recommend to the Congress the submission of a constitutional amendment on equal rights for women."

The National Committee to Defeat the Unequal Rights Amendment

Alarmed by the successes of ERA advocates, especially the platform victories and fearing a Senate vote, the Women's Bureau coalition called a meeting in September 1944 "to organise a National Directing Committee to oppose the Equal Rights Amendment." Twenty-seven groups decided to coalesee under the rubric of the "National Committee to Defeat the UnEqual Rights Amendment" (NCDURA). The membership consisted principally of labour organisations and the national women's organisations making up the Women's Bureau coalition. NCDURA decided that in addition to lobbying against the ERA, it would set up local branches in each state to combat the ERA directly and to undermine its support by eliminating discriminatory state laws. Because even members of this committee could not agree on which laws genuinely discriminated against women, that determination was left up to the state organisations. By June 1945 fifteen state committees had been formed, and the group, which had initially planned to operate for only six months, decided to continue functioning "until the end of the emergency." NCDRUA's roster was a veritable roll call of liberal organisations, now comprising forty-three national organisations, including the American Civil Liberties Union.

Although advocacy of individual rights had become identified, since the New Deal, with the liberal wing of the democratic party, support for the Equal Rights Amendment in Congress came mostly from Republicans and conservative Democrats from the South and the Southwest. On its face, the ERA was appealing—after all, it mandated equal treatment under law for half the population. Opposition to it, rather than support of it, required explanation, especially now that both parties had endorsed it. In their own defense, opponents cited the threat to protective labour laws; but those legislators who were indifferent to the labour law question had little reason to contest their party's official position. So probusiness Republicans and antilabour Southern Democrats found themselves on the same side of the issue. Advocacy of the Equal Rights Amendment served, too, as a defense against the accusation that the South opposed civil rights: some Southern legislators held that equality for white women ought to come before, or at the very least with, equality for black men and women. Some liberals accepted the argument that women deserved constitutional equality and that government regulation of the workplace could extend to both men and women workers. The array of arguments concerning the ERA resulted in peculiar alliances on the issue: both the vigorously liberal Claude Pepper, a Democratic senator from Florida, and the ultraconservative Howard W. Smith, a Democratic representative from Virginia, favoured the amendment. But in general, conservatives, finding the arguments in favour of free enterprise and individual opportunity especially appealing, tended to favour the amendment, whereas liberals, who espoused the idea that government had a positive responsibility to protect women and the family through regulation, were more likely to oppose the ERA.

For the moment, ERA advocates continued to carry the day. Citing the party platform pledges, the House Judiciary Committee in July 1945 reported the amendment favourably (by a vote of fifteen to seven) for the first time since its introduction twenty-one years before. The NWP's revelation of support from Cardinal Dennis Dougherty "caused a minor sensation" in the Senate subcommittee hearing and, primed by vigilant lobbying on the part of NWP workers, it voted in favour of the ERA four to one.

In an effort to queli the tide of support, Frances Perkins urged President Truman to meet with the opponents of the ERA; he agreed to see them in September. In 1944 then Senator Truman had written to Emma Guffey Miller: "I am in sympathy with [the] fight for the Equal Rights Amendment because I think it will improve the standard of living." Despite Miller's entreaties, however, Truman had not reiterated his favourable statement. Now confronted with a contingent of well-known liberal women, Truman was hardly willing to disavow his support for protective labour legislation. Administration aides trying to craft a position for the president felt besieged. "This is a tough baby," presidential aide William Hassett observed to David Niles, an administrative assistant. Niles concurred: "This Equal Rights thing is dynamite which ever way you place it." Matthew Connelly, the president's secretary, finally signed the letter to NCDURA chair Dorothy McAllister. The president, he wrote, "plans to give some thought to the Equal Rights Amendment in the near future and is grateful for the careful analysis you have made of this problem." Aware that the issue was both complex and charged, President Truman issued no further public statements for or against the Equal Rights Amendment.

The Senate Judiciary Committee, voting eleven to four, reported the ERA favourably on January 21, 1946. The measure now stood ready for a vote in both houses of Congress.

Supporters and opponents lobbied vigorously. Under the letterhead of the Industrial League for Equality (an NWP creation designed to suggest labour support for the amendment), Congress members received a copy of a 1913 editorial by American Federation of Labour president Samuel Gompers asserting that the "industrial problems of women are not isolated, but inextricably associated with those of men." An excerpt from the Supreme Court's 1941 decision upholding the Fair Labour Standards Act noted that hours and wage laws could now safely be applied to both men and women. The other side sent a letter opposing the amendment, signed by Eleanor Roosevelt, Frances Perkins, Carrie Chapman Catt (the leader of the National American Women Suffrage Association when the suffrage amendment was ratified), and several other notable American women.

When the roll was called in the Senate on July 19, 1946, the amendment won a majority—thirty-eight to thirty-five—but not the two-thirds majority needed for victory. With twenty-three of the favourable votes Republican, plus two absentee Republicans recorded in favour, the total was one shy of two-thirds of the thirty-nine Republican senators. Democrats made up fifteen of the pro votes, with two absent Democrats indicating their approval as well, accounting for less than a third of the fifty-six Senate Democrats. Only four of the assenting Democrats were from states outside the South or Southwest.

Crushed by the loss, the NWP complained that the vote had come without advance notice, when several pro-ERA senators were away from Washington. But opponent Senator Carl Hayden (D-Ariz.) insisted that many ERA supporters had voted in favour only because they knew the measure would fail. The conflict had taken a toll, as later events showed: it was long before support gained such strength again. Several senators had promised that they would not vote in favour of the amendment in the future, NCDURA informed its membership, now that they knew more about its implications. The *New York Times* expressed its pleasure in an editorial: "Motherhood cannot be amended, and we are glad the Senate didn't try." The measure never came to a vote in the House.

The *Times* righdy marked motherhood as the central issue. The failure of the ERA hinged not on the chance absence of its supporters but on the unwillingness of the nation as a whole to affirm the independent equality of women at a moment when the restoration of "normal" family life constituted a pre-eminent objective. Still reeling from wartime and conversion upheaval, with industry unsettled by strikes and families fighting inflation, equal treatment for women in the public sphere seemed beside the point. Women were needed at home.

But the impulse that had led to the ERA vote could not be entirely submerged. Both equity and the place women had gained in the workforce supported the call for some response from the federal government. The battle over the ERA went on through the next decade, a metaphor for the largely unacknowledged struggle being waged as women attempted to reconcile their home and public lives. For activist women in Washington, the amendment continued to dominate the political scene, generating alternative legislative proposals, all of which suffered from the difficulty of coming to terms with the changing role of women.

10

Political Strategies and Outcomes

The liberal politics of the Kennedy administration, embodied particularly in the President's Commission on the Status of Women, gave shape to the agenda of the first feminist organisation of the 1960s and provided it with both a structural and a psychological underpinning. New administrations, particularly when a new party takes over, bring bursts of energy to the political process. If after the dislocations of World War II the populace had sought a return to stability, fifteen years later Kennedy's call to action tapped a wellspring of enthusiasm for solving social problems. Although no grassroots women's movement pressed for them, new frontiers opened for women.

The Equal Rights Amendment

Ambivalence about women's roles in the postwar period had shown themselves in national politics in the battle over several legislative initiatives. The most important measure to be entangled in these complex feelings was the Equal Rights Amendment, which served as context for most of the other legislative disputes concerning women.

The Equal Rights Amendment failed because federal policymakers would hardly approve so significant a proposal without wide and deep support for it. An amendment to grant women constitutional equality bespoke a belief in the right of women to function as individuals. But individual equality, however in keeping it was with traditional American ideals, conflicted with an ideology that considered women as responsible primarily to their families, not to themselves. Historically, the law defined women as wives, mothers, and daughters, placing them under the aegis of their husbands and fathers. Twentieth-century innovations gave the state a new role in overseeing the conditions of women's employment, under the rationale of protecting their interests as homemakers. The Equal Rights Amendment, which would remove legal distinctions between the sexes, suggested a reordering of the world, a responsibility the U.S. Congress does not readily assume. By 1960, women leaders had had little to show for their efforts except token offerings of executive appointments, tendered by presidents who were staying out of the fray.

Token Appointments

The strategy of token appointments offered many advantages to the presidents who employed it. The women's organisations on both sides of the ERA struggle emphasised their desire for more appointments of women, persuaded that such appointments marked significant gains for the sex. Thus, presidents who followed that course won praise, especially from women journalists, who found the selections made good copy. Appointments, moreover, could be had at virtually no cost, and they were easy to effect. Unless the candidate was wildly unqualified (and women appointees tended to be overqualified), the Senate offered no opposition to a presidential choice. In many cases, Senate confirmation was not even required.

But welcomed as they were by women's organisations, the appointments had an unanticipated consequence that worked badly for women seeking substantive measures. By acceding to the request for more women appointees, the chief executive could evade much more significant policy questions. The president could state in truth to his women constituents that he had met *one* of their objectives; he could not in fairness be asked to meet them all, especially when no political pressure existed outside Washington for a comprehensive programme for women. Therefore, the groups requesting appointments diminished their chances of wresting other—more important—benefits from the administration.

Moreover, the willingness of chief executives to yield to these requests itself suggested that the appointments made little difference for the status of most women. In general, when the standing of a particular group has been low, it has often sought high-level appointments as a way of winning respect and recognition, and the symbolic value of a black or female cabinet officer may in fact have important psychological and sociological implications. But in the absence of a social movement to enhance the position of blacks or women, such token appointees can achieve few concrete gains. In order to prove the competence of both the group and the officeholder, a token appointee is constrained to "lean over backward", as Mary Anderson observed of Frances Perkins, not to show favouritism and thereby lose credibility with the white males who made the appointment. The ability of such a woman official in the postwar period to assist the underprivileged members of her group was thus severely limited. In fact, the onus on the appointee was to prove that she was no different from the usual nominee. Under these circumstances, only an executive whose job expressly required her to address the status of women felt free to press for meaningful change.

When John Kennedy was elected president, he sought programmes that would directly address the problems American society confronted in the 1960s. A well-developed programme concerning women—one that comported with his views and the rest of his liberal agenda and that had few political costs—emerged from the Women's Bureau coalition. Kennedy's ties to the progressive labour community made him especially receptive to the coalition's plan of action (as Truman's ties to the Democratic National Convention had made him sympathetic to its agenda). Kennedy's appointment of Esther Peterson to head the Women's Bureau and then to assume the post of assistant secretary of labour placed a representative of the women's Bureau coalition in a highly strategic position. With access to the president and to all the political resources of the administration, close ties to her own constituency, and an impressive degree of political savvy, Peterson proved to be an effective agent for the Women's Bureau coalition, providing leadership and crafting compromises.

The President's Commission on the Status of Women

The programme of the Women's Bureau spoke to the unresolved problems in women's lives, and the President's Commission on the Status of Women was its centrepiece. Emerging in part from the animus of the Women's Bureau coalition against the ERA, the commission succeeded in undermining the amendment. But its role was not merely negative. Peterson, Arthur Goldberg, and John Kennedy recognised the hardships caused by the injustices that the ERA sought to correct. Women were often denied the right to serve on juries; some states gave husbands total control of family income or barred women from certain professions; the right to contract, own, and convey property or to establish domicile was available to women only within limits. In addition, women in the labour force consistently earned lower wages than did men, and they had fewer opportunities for advancement. Even the adversaries of constitutional equality recognised the need to better women's condition.

Using models provided by the civil rights movement (federal commissions, legislation, executive orders) and drawing on the same liberal ideology of individual equality, these advocates for women's rights—at a time of continuing ambivalence about appropriate roles for women—addressed many of the legal and extralegal inequities women's traditional roles, and the tension between this ideal and the simultaneous quest for expanded opportunities for women as paid workers pervaded all the commission's discussions and recommendations. At the same time, however, the commission also conferred new respect on the subject of equality for women, and it forged into one agenda the proposals of the three diverse groups fighting for women's opportunities: the proponents of constitutional equality, the advocates of increased opportunity in the workplace, and those who sought appointments for women.

At its conclusion in 1963, the commission proposed, and President Kennedy established, two continuing federal bodies to monitor action on the status of women. State legislatures and governors followed the presidential model and instituted their own commissions on the status of women, developing a national network of women and men knowledgeable and concerned about the position of women in society.

When ERA supporters succeeding in adding to the Civil Rights Act of 1964 a provision protecting the employment rights of women, many women activists responded with hesitation because of the conflict between women's role in the labour force and their responsibilities in the home, which the presidents commission had left unresolved. But the disdain with which the Equal Employment Opportunity Commission treated its obligation to enforce this section of the law catalysed the network created by the presidential commission of those involved in women's issues and led to the formation of the first women's rights group of the new wave of feminism, the National Organisation for Women.

Possibilities and Limitations of Government Action

Presidential commissions are commonly thought to be worse than useless. A rhyme that appeared in *Punch* in the 1950s expresses the common view:

If you're pestered by critics and hounded by faction
To take some precipitate, positive action,
The proper procedure, to take my advice, is
Appoint a commission and stave off the crisis.

Herbert Hoover admitted creating "a dozen committees" in order to divert crusaders into research.

Yet presidential commissions have often resulted in worthwhile outcomes. They have built support for controversial courses of action, helped to provide data to back up proposals for mainstream legislation, dramatised the existence of problem, and broken policy deadlocks. Thomas R. Wolanin, investigating the policy achievements of presidential advisory commissions from Harry Truman through Richard Nixon, concluded that 68 percent of presidential commissions produced "substantial" or "major" presidential responses to their recommendations, and 59 percent elicited "substantial" or "major" responses from federal government agencies.

The experience with the President's Commission on the Status of Women sustains Wolanin's thesis that commissions can meaningfully affect issues. The president's commission and its state-level offspring helped to legitimise the issue of sex discrimination, made data available to support allegations that discrimination against women constituted a serious problem, drew up agendas to ameliorate inequities, raised expectations that responsible parties would take action, and, most important, sensitised a nationwide network of women to the problems women faced. This network proved to be in the vanguard of the creation of the widespread, vocal women's movement that surfaced at the end of the 1960s. Betty Friedan, the first president of the National Organisation for Women, repeatedly acknowledged the model the president's commission had provided for NOW, although she expressed disappointment with the commission's accomplishments. The change in approach from highly publicised but ephemeral token appointments to a presidential commission proved beneficial.

The initiatives of the Kennedy administration anticipated, rather than responded to, the appearance of a broad-based feminist movement and ultimately helped to bring it about. Characterised by the quest not for fundamental change but for attainable goals, this significant policy shift occurred despite the absence of a grassroots movement seeking federal action.

If the fate of women's issues in the Kennedy administration demonstrates that representatives of interest groups can initiate significant policy change, it also indicates the limits of such a course of action. The president's commission proposed moderate steps, placing the responsibility for implementation on government and private institutions. But none of these institutions had strong incentives to execute the proposals on their own, and Congress was loath to establish new bureaucracies to control private business. New bureaucracies cost money and make people angry; employers are important campaign contributors and vigilant lobbyists. Without political pressure, legislation would be hard to come by. So the temperate federal steps taken as the result of internal policy pressures engendered expectations the federal government did not intend to fulfil.

Jo Freeman has pointed out that policy is "the means by which government stimulate[s], respond[s] to, and/or curtail[s] social change." It represents an attempt to channel or preempt the conflict. Yet policy can also incite reformers. By collecting information and offering modest solutions, the federal government helped to turn a latent issue into a salient one and to supply data to those who wanted to go further than the government did. In order to justify even limited steps, the president's commission and the Women's Bureau had gathered copious evidence to substantiate their proposals so that they could persuade Congress and other political actors to respond appropriately. By doing so, they pointed out problems of which the general populace had before been largely unaware. The minimal change the federal government supported could not have eliminated the pervasive problem it documented. So the government action heightened awareness, raised expectations, and then disappointed the new observers.

But in order to achieve an effective and coherent government policy concerning women's issues, women activists had not only to resolve internal contradictions within their own groups but also to reach a rapproachement with other women's organisations. The philosophies of the National Women's party and the Women's Bureau represented thesis and antithesis—two sides of the ambivalent attitude toward women in the postwar period—but a new resolution or restatement of the problem was essential if a united front was to be presented to policy makers.

That resolution grew out of the changing status of women, but it was also made possible by an ideological leap—new feminist theory separated childbearing from childraising, philosophically if not in fact, and permitted a redefinition of the "problem" of women's status. Without such a resolution, policy makers could have continued to exploit the differences in the views of women. Once NOW adopted the position that both mothers and fathers were responsible for the care of children, a coherent feminist philosophy could inform responses to questions of policy.

The new women's movement was also able to move beyond the president's commission because by now the remedies the Commission had recommended had been tried and found wanting. As halfway measures proved inadequate, those who previously had hesitated now came to acknowledge the need for potent curatives. The National Organisation for Women quickly became aware that the proposals of the president's commission, based as they were on traditional conceptions of sex roles, had no power to get at the root causes of discrimination. The group's endorsement of the Equal Rights Amendment soon followed. Thus the president's commission, formed in part to ward off the ERA, unintentionally contributed both to its endorsement by virtually every liberal group that once had opposed it and to the recognition that the sex roles on which special legislation for women had been based had limited utility for the final three decades of the twentieth century. As Sara

Evans remarked: "The purpose, in fact, may have been to quell a growing pressure for an Equal Rights Amendment, but unwittingly the government organised its own opposition." And Frances Kolb has observed: "The network's realisation of the need for action collided with the inaction of the government agencies producing the classic revolutionary situation in which the revolution began in the government's backyard, at a government sponsored event!"

Not only did federal activity assist in the development of the women's movement, it made it more broad based. The vigour of the women's movement came partly from its solid roots in traditional liberal politics. Both at its inception and at its height, the women's movement at the national level operated largely in the context of prevailing values and institutions. It was at its most effective when it sought incremental changes, involving equality of individual opportunity, the central tenet of liberal theory. Moderate demands cloaked the magnitude of fundamental change that took place whenever women *were* viewed by the government as individuals rather than as instruments of the family.

The array of feminist organisations formed by middle-class women in addition to the community-based groups formed by younger, more radical women, provided women across the country a site of activity on as broad or narrow a range of issues as they wished. In time, the distinctions between "radical" and "middle-class" feminists became less clear. Historically, radical organisations have not been successful in the United States, which is a system organised to sustain the politics of the centre. Jo Freeman has observed that, whereas the political system rewards those who seek reform, it excludes proponents of fundamental change. Yet, ironically, the mainstream women's organisations, such as NOW, have advocated one of the most fundamental changes in American life.

In short, the women who became federal policy makers during an era in which they themselves eschewed the term *feminist* ultimately helped to bring about a revitalisation of feminism—to create, in the words of James Q. Wilson, an "enduring organisational base" for influencing policy. These leaders, without a women's movement to back them up, forced the federal government to recognise that changes were taking place in women's lives, and they shaped the government's response. Ultimately—predictably—demands outstripped the possibilities of ready government acquiescence.

The presidential commission's report came at a critical moment. As Ethel Klein has documented, women were poised to expand their roles in the world. Between 1960 and 1970 the fertility rate declined from 118 per thousand to 87.9: mothers with preschool children increased their labour force participation rate from 19 percent to 30 percent; and the divorce rate rose from 15 per thousand women to 26 per thousand. In 1966, the cumulative efforts of the President's Commission on the Status of Women and the federal agencies it spawned, the state commissions on women, ERA activists, and women both inside and outside the government culminated in the emergence of an independent women's movement. In December 1967, the *New York Times* alerted its readers to the fact that "the feminists are on the march once more."

Feminism

The feminism of the late sixties and seventies reaffirmed the philosophy that men and women should be politically, economically, and socially equal, but it also expanded the theory to argue that differences between men's and women's roles were culturally based rather than biologically determined. In practical terms, this new definition released women, at least in principle, from the total responsibility for childcare. It also meant that, for the first time, feminism was an internally consistent ideology, no longer rent by the contradictory demands for both equality and special privileges for women as mothers. Although consideration would still be requested for those who took care of children, now these "privileges" would be sought for male parents as well as for female ones, and employers would find that both men and women had demands on them as parents as well as workers.

Before this ideological break took place, women who fought for women struggled fruitlessly to resolve the central dilemma of women's lives: how to be at once an individual concerned with her own destiny *and* a mother (no word evokes a more laden image) entirely responsible for the welfare of her children. Some called themselves "feminists", and some did not.

Because the definition of feminism has changed, historians today writing about the history of feminism face problems. The term *feminism* is now as much normative as it is descriptive. We find it difficult to conclude that Eleanor Roosevelt, a great woman in every sense of the term, was not a feminist (a word she never would have applied to herself). So modern works often begin with a set of definitions that permit the writer to apply the label "feminist" as she or he sees fit. But the profusion of definitions is at once confusing and unnecessary. The term *feminism* as we use it was born in the 1960s. We need not ask if women were "feminists" *per se* in order to comprehend their behaviour and motivation, or to illuminate their character. To do so, in fact, can create a diversion and may, because of the emotional content of the term, distort a view point rather than clarify it.

Instead, we might ask: Which elements of women's lives appeared to a historical figure to be immutable? What aspects of women's lives did she or he question? What beliefs informed a choice of action? Did an activist favour a wider range of influence for women, or more power within a narrow one? How did class origins colour political agendas? What constraints limited the selection of political strategies?

Effectives Strategies

For the purposes of this study, I have distinguished among activist women by describing the strategies they promoted. My pursuit has been to determine which strategies proved effective under which conditions. Governmental responses to social change do alter outcomes, although not necessarily in predictable or desirable ways. Political decisions can intensify, or retard, nascent social movements. Good strategies push the political system as far as possible without provoking a backlash, making the best of even inhospitable times. The story of policy for women in the premovement era suggests some approaches. In the absence of a strong social movement, we find that posing an all-or-nothing choice results in no gain at all. Conversely, incremental goals often can be achieved. If a group succeeds in gaining access to the White House, executive actions are easier to come by than legislative ones, but successful proposals are virtually always noncontroversial ones with low political costs. Neither a quest for appointments nor devotion to a single nonnegotiable legislative measure is likely to be productive. Compromises, in contrast, can elicit meaningful, if incomplete, initial efforts that can later lead to more effective policy instruments. The lesson is in fact an old one: If you want to get a camel into someone's tent, ask if you can just put its nose under the tentflap.

Index